# Explosive Athlete

## Jump Higher, Run Faster...
## ...Perform Better

By

## Jason Shea and Farren Davis

# Table of Contents

# Chapter 1

# *Jump Higher, Run Faster*

### *"How do you determine who gets the scholarship?"*

This was the question asked we asked a Top 10 (*at the time*) College Football program recruiting director back in 2006 during personal conversation.

His response was not only eye opening, but it also provided valuable insight into the way athletes needed to train.

He expressed that once the coaches had seen and analyzed an athlete's game film, the two most important things he looked at in an athlete were:

1. **How high and athlete could jump**
2. **How the athlete treated their mother during the recruiting meeting.**

Oftentimes, the athletes who can either jump the highest in the vertical jump or the furthest in the standing broad jump, are nearly always the best performers in acceleration and short sprint tests.

In all our personal experience with testing agility, oftentimes the athletes with the best pound for pound front squat and power clean (or high pull) were almost always the best performers in the 5-10-5.

A 2015 study on professional league Rugby players found that dominant leg lateral jump performance was a major predictor in change of direction tests (4).

Several studies have shown that ***those who performed better in vertical jump, squat jumps, 1 and/or 2 legged-broad jumps, and drop jumps had significantly better performances in short linear sprint tests*** (1,5,6,8,9,10,13).

A 2016 study on Division I college soccer players found significant relationships between specific jump tests and sprint distances (7):

- **0–5 m sprint:**
  - Strong relationship with Vertical Jump, Unilateral and Bilateral Standing Broad Jump, and the left-leg Triple Hop test.
  - Significant relationship with the right-leg Triple Hop.
- **0–10 m sprint:**
  - Strong relationship between both left- and right-leg Standing Broad Jump
  - Stronger relationship with Vertical Jump, Standing Broad Jump, and left-leg Triple Hop.
  - Near-perfect relationship with right-leg Triple Hop.
- **0–30 m sprint:**
  - Strong relationship between both left- and right-leg Standing Broad Jump
  - Stronger relationship between Vertical Jump, Standing Broad Jump, and both Left and Right Leg Triple Hop. were documented with VJ, SBJ and left- and right-leg TH.

A more recent study tested 12 college basketball players in the vertical jump, standing broad jump, and 2-step approach jump while measuring average and peak power of each. The researchers then compared the results of these tests to a series of on-court sprint tests including 10 meter and ¾ court sprints, yo-yo intermittent recovery test, and pro-agility test.

They found a **strong correlation between approach jump and pro-agility as well as ¾-court sprint performances, while the vertical, broad jump, and peak power correlated with 10 meter sprint performance** (3).

## Structural Balance and Injury Prevention

An athlete's structural balance also plays a role in these field tests. While working for *a top* 10 JUCO football team *(Dean Junior College)* and national runner-up men's rugby team *(Boston Irish Wolfhounds)*, we were challenged to predict *"the most athletic"* players just by looking at testing results. The coaches had challenged us to pick their most athletic players based on the results of 6 non field/non-sprinting evaluations.

The six tests we used were:

- Overhead Squat evaluation
- Klatt test
- 1-1.5m/s "ass to the grass" back squat relative to bodyweight
- Power clean from hang just above the knee relative to body weight
- Vertical Jump
- Single leg standing broad jump

**The combined scoring for those tests strongly correlated with the players 10yd sprint, 40yd sprint, 5-10-5 (pro-agility), T-test, and Illinois drill.**

There were outliers, of course, as some athletes were great top speed, linear sprinters with reactive/elastic ability to spare. Some of these outliers did not perform well in the strength and power tests. A few even a few struggled in the overhead squat eval, as struggled with tight hips and hamstrings.

With their fast twitch dominance, these athletes had great potential for improvement - as most of them had little experience in Olympic lifts, proper plyometric training, nor how to land, cut, or decelerate / accelerate efficiently. One wrong cut at high velocity could mean the difference between a game breaking play and spending the rest of the season on the sidelines.

## The Cost of Injury

The out-of-pocket cost of an ACL injury in the US ranges from about $500-$3000, with a lifetime cost of up to $80,000 in some non-surgical / rehab-only situations. This does not include the time missed from sport or daily activities, never mind the psychological effects of any major injury (14).

Over 200,000 ACL injuries occur in the US per year, with the majority of patients electing to undergo surgical repair / intervention. The goal being full restoration of joint mobility and strength, with the hopes of effective return-to-sport and avoidance of arthritis. This usually follows training and a battery of testing protocols to ensure safety.

Surgery is between **$500-$3000** out of pocket, after insurance.

Lifetime cost of up to **$80,000**

Over **200,000 ACL injuries** in the US per year

With this in mind, what happens when an athlete returns too soon or has not completely restored functional capacity? Is there a concern for re-injury?

A recent study reported higher re-injury rates and osteoarthritis in those electing operative reconstruction (15).

**Some researchers see re-tear / re-injury 15x more likely within the first 12 months post-surgery. Re-injury in existing ACLR patients was 6x greater within 24 months than those without an existing ACL injury** (16). This data may provide evidence that there may be a need to push for longer wait times after the reconstruction has taken place. The problem is, will this work for the typical high school, college, or even Olympic athlete (*all operating with 4 years of competition / training*) to enjoy a successful sport career?

Most of the published information has been leading to the conclusion that the longer the rehab and post-surgical wait period, the better. The problem is this may not be an option for the competitive athlete's schedule.

The most recent reviews on the preventative aspects of ACL injury points to the effectiveness of neuromuscular training intervention. This aspect can be seen firsthand at cutting edge sports-medicine clinics that are now connected with Injury Prevention / Strength and Conditioning centers.

While isolated muscle tests once reigned supreme in the screening return-to-play process, jumping, bounding and tests of functional strength and power have come to the forefront. These tests may ensure the athlete is not only at a decreased risk of injury/re-injury, but is also performing at a high functional level, and perhaps, in some cases, even more explosive than pre-injury levels.

**The 6 principles of an effective injury prevention program** (17), based off the research included:

1. Intervention at an early age
2. Biomechanics and movement efficiency
3. Consistency and compliance with the training program
4. Dosage of training
5. Feedback and good coaching!
6. Variety of exercises

**CHEAT SHEET: Passing the ACL test for Athletes returning to play:**
*This is always graft and athlete specific of course*

**Ensuring adequate hamstring : quadriceps strength ratio**, while not the most functional – this does show a deficit to train after. While these are often trained, don't leave out extensive training to strengthen Adductor and groin muscles as well as the hips.

**Balance testing** – using the Y-balance test has proven to be a great screening tool of overall foot / arch stability, while also revealing hip limitations, also allows us to see deficiency:
- Standing on a center block with 1 leg
- Push a separate block as far away as you can without losing balance
- Perform the same push of that block to the back side at 45degrees away from the hip, and back across the body of the standing leg.

**Explosive Strength and Jumping / Landing ability:**
- Performing single leg broad jumps, don't be afraid to land on 2 legs in training, but single leg landings reveal the most for further strength improvements
- Diagonal bounding abilities should be trained and tested, including simple single-leg triple-hop with single-leg landings as a gold standard (see the differences in control and power from injured/non-injured legs
- Reflexive ankle / knee / hip integrity – often times this is tested as a single leg hop for time (usually 6meters) – but athletes should not be afraid to train this by jump rope variations

Performance in these tests or drills paints a picture of how an athlete can decelerate, change direction, dive, tackle, chase, elude, or run through an opponent.

**Speaking of "running through opponents"**

To take the testing even further, we attempted to correlate who the heaviest hitters on the teams would be. After spending a week at a Poliquin Performance seminar at the Leicester Tigers Rugby team training center, it became apparent in observing the training of high level Rugby players, that performance in certain exercises could correlate to an athlete's ability to dole out physical punishment.

The athletes who were the best at certain exercises were nearly always those were able to turn themselves into human battering rams, always driving through tackles. They expressed true movement integrity, making it appear effortless through the external forces against them.

This not only applied to football and Rugby, but in testing and training thousands of athletes across the board, we saw these same correlations in hockey, lacrosse, and basketball. *(Wrestling had its own unique correlations with some crossover).*

The tackling sport athletes who were often the most feared *"hitters"* were the best at:

- Heavy tire flips (500lbs +)
- 10-20yd Super Yoke (relative to bodyweight)
- Deadlift
- Power clean from the hang above the knee

- Hamstrings to calves Front Squat (relative to bodyweight)
- "Ass to the grass" 1-1.5m/s back squat (relative to bodyweight)

Oftentimes, these athletes guys excelled in either one or both of the modified strongman exercises (Heavy Tire Flips and Super Yoke), and near the tops on their team relative to bodyweight in at least 2 of the strength exercises *(tight hips in back squat depth and grip strength in the deadlift could be limiting factors.)*

One of the more memorable workouts we witnessed a heavy hitting inside/outside center on the Tigers doing was:

| Exercise | Reps | Sets | Tempo | Rest |
| --- | --- | --- | --- | --- |
| A1: Heavy Tire Flips | 2 | 10 | NA | 0s |
| A2: 15-20yd Backward Sled Drag | 15-20yd | 10 | NA | 0s |
| A3: Heavy Tire Slips | 2 | 10 | NA | 0s |
| A4: 15-20yd Backward Sled Drag | 15-20yd | 10 | NA | 120s |

In his excellent book *Strongman Training for Sport*, Charles Poliquin and Art McDermott provided a similar workout, substituting Super Yoke burst for the sled drag. One version of that we used at *APECS* with high level college and high school football athletes was:

| Exercise | Reps | Sets | Tempo | Rest |
| --- | --- | --- | --- | --- |
| A1: 10yd Super Yoke Carry | 10yds | 10 | NA | 0s |
| A2: Heavy Tire Flips | 2 | 10 | NA | 0s |
| A3: 10yd Super Yoke Carry | 10yds | 10 | NA | 0s |
| A4: Heavy Tire Flips | 15-20yd | 10 | NA | 120-180 |

Other modified strongman variations included:

| Exercise | Reps | Sets | Tempo | Rest |
|---|---|---|---|---|
| A1: Heavy Tire Flips | 2 | 10 | NA | 0s |
| A2: 10yd Prowler Acceleration | 10yd | 10 | NA | 90s |
| B1: 20yd Farmer Carry | 20yd | 6 | NA | 0s |
| B2: 15-20yd Backward Sled Drag | 15-20yd | 6 | NA | 90s |

Or

| Exercise | Reps | Sets | Tempo | Rest |
|---|---|---|---|---|
| A1: Heavy Tire Flips | 2 | 6 | NA | 0s |
| A2: Log Push Press | 3-5 | 6 | 10X1 | 90s |
| B1: 20s Tire Battle | 20yd | 6 | NA | 0s |
| B2: 2" Diameter Rope Hand Over Hand Rope Pull | 1 | 6 | NA | 90s |

Or

| Exercise | Reps | Sets | Tempo | Rest |
|---|---|---|---|---|
| A1: Super Yoke | 10-15yds | 6 | NA | 10s-20s |
| A2: Farmer Carry | 15-20yd | 6 | NA | 120-180s |
| B1: Overhead Kettlebell Throws | 3-4 | 6 | NA | 10s-20s |
| B2: Hand Over Hand Atlas Stone Push (in sand or uphill) | 5-7s | 6 | NA | 120s |

Given the constant variation of loading and variable resistance in strongman training, it is not only a great tool for increasing functional strength and performance, but it is also a potential tool *(modified of course)* for rehab. With his work at The Micheli Center for Sports Injury Prevention, coach Davis has seen it used in countless ACL return-to-play programs once the athletes have been cleared to train.

The variation of exercises acts to stimulate the nervous system in such a way that it prepares the body for rapid changes of direction and loading due to awkward carrying positions, differing step-rates and total body irradiation of tension. It allows trainees to incorporate even the smallest stabilization muscles for big compound all-out efforts, with minimal joint impact.

Certain modified strongman movements can also be useful for the beginning stages of rehab as they may restore functional strength levels and muscle hypertrophy much faster than traditional machine-based isolation exercises.

An example of a late-rehab stages of an **ACL-Return-to-Play program** may use this **Beginner Strongman Medley** to build general physical preparedness. This particular program was used with a 13 y/o female high school basketball player who had anterior knee pain following a patella-graft 9 months prior to training. With 160-240 yards of drag and carry volume, the main emphasis was repeated effort conditioning of the total body.

| Exercise | Reps | Sets | Tempo | Rest |
|---|---|---|---|---|
| A1: 40yd Backward Sled Drag | 40yds | 4-6 | NA | 0s |
| A1: 40yd Farmers-carry | 40yds | 4-6 | NA | 0s |
| A2: 40yd Lateral Sled Drag | 40yds | 4-6 | NA | 0s |
| A3: 40yd Overhead Barbell Carry | 40yds | 4-6 | NA | 120-180s |

In this ACL-Return-To-Play program the 40yd backward sled drag is for the specific overload and re-introduction of the patella surrounding musculature of the quadriceps (specifically the Vastus Medialis). This allows for integration into complex movements while also maintaining postural control (*an often overlooked but major factor in agility*).

The 40yd farmer carry provides upright stability training and integrates gait and high marching mechanics. The 40yd lateral sled drag introduces sport specific lateral speed development without the joint impact of running. The cross-over step and power-step push off movements increase the drive from the hip abductor and adductor muscles.

The 40yd overhead barbell carry integrates the overhead push pattern with dynamic postural control. It also keeps the metabolic demand high with marching or walking under a load.

Hang weights from a superband - off a barbell or when grasped this can tend to twirl / bounce / jolt in multiple directions which helps to pull and push the athlete off course through the simple task of walking or marching

The circuit of exercises provides conditioning, but more importantly it also gets a high rep count with different variations of walking and marching. The rapid turnover and foot contacts under load seen in drags and carries are great reconditioning tools for a more robust and resilient athletes following injury.

## A quick word about structural balance

Coach Davis grew up as a roofer, installing shingle, metal, or slate roofing on any structure from small houses to large barns. One constant reminder from his boss at the time, who happened to be his father, was that of the 1000's of overlapping pieces, if just one piece was wrong or insecure, the whole roof would be compromised.

They always started from the bottom up, layer upon layer, allowing water and snow to run down off the roof. This prevented water from being backed up or penetrating below the surface. The job was not complete until the entire roof was covered and void of leaks. The same can be said for the body, with regards to energy leaks.

**Building a house vs building an athlete:** Instead of lumber, plumbing, and wiring, the athlete requires layers of stability, strength, conditioning, power, then speed.

When driving by any building construction site, steel beams, re-bar, and concrete are all visible staples of the landscape. Each of these plays a vital role in the stability of the structural framework of a building. For example, if the placement or level of just one beam or re-bar is not precise, the stability of the entire framework becomes compromised. The musculoskeletal system of the human body is no different.

19

Negative health consequences ranging from chronic pain to acute injury can result from these faults in one's framework. According to a 2008 study out of the prestigious *British Journal of Medicine*, most ACL tears in adolescents and young adults occurred while participating in sports (12), with female athletes at a five-fold greater risk than their male counterparts (11).

The concept of structural balance is the brainchild of renowned strength coach Charles Poliquin. After training thousands of athletes at all levels of sports Olympic and Professional, coach Poliquin noticed trends between athletic performance and optimal strength ratios between agonist, antagonist, and synergistic muscle groups. Understanding that the body is only as strong as its weakest link, he addressed these weak links in order to reach an athlete's full potential.

Oftentimes when extensive attention is paid to one muscle group at the expense of others, muscular imbalances may occur. The overworked muscle may become shortened while its antagonist becomes lengthened and weak. For example, the muscles you see when looking in a mirror, chest, abs, and biceps, often receive more training attention than their less visible counterparts, the external rotators, back, and triceps.

An overemphasis on these anterior muscles, in addition to a lack of proper training for their antagonists may lead to an increased potential for injury. During one lecture former

Olympian and now track and field strength coach Dan John gave a very simple example of this. He expressed that if we contract and flex our abs, biceps, and pec muscles, we create the forward rounded hunchback posture. Instantly we have created the aging posture of an 80-year old versus an athletic 20-something.

Pete Egoscue of the *Egoscue Method* has said this rounded forward posture is gravity trying to pull us over into the letter C.

Another common muscular imbalance, attributable to extended periods of sitting, is tight hip flexors and inhibited hip extensors. When a muscle becomes chronically shortened and overactive, in this case the hip flexors, the motor cortex part of the brain sends neuro-inhibitory signals to the antagonist telling it to relax or stand down.

This phenomenon is referred to as reciprocal inhibition. With reciprocal inhibition, there may also be an over-reliance on the assistive, or synergistic, muscles, further exacerbating any structural imbalances.

If the anterior deltoid and chest muscles are so tight it actually rolls the scapula upward and the head of the humerus forward out of its previously centered alignment. With this the full array of joint stabilizers, known as the rotator cuff, is pulled out of the optimal position unable to do its job properly.

When the shoulder joint is not centered this creates difficult environment to get stronger. This due to the lack of proper stabilization at the base level of movements like the barbell bench press. A lack of posterior strength / stability is likely inhibiting the ability to produce more force.

To assess structural balance, specific strength-based exercises and movement screens are used to test for imbalances throughout the entire musculoskeletal chain. The movement screens assess lower body function and muscular balance, while the strength tests assess ratios between (X) upper body and (Y) lower body exercises.

For example, optimal structural balance of the shoulder girdle is reflected by the ability to perform eight repetitions in the seated dumbbell external rotator exercise with roughly 10% of a trainee's one repetition max in the flat barbell bench press.

Some positions limit the body's natural ability to create and/or express explosive strength and power. These can be the muscle groups that are emphasized in some strength and conditioning programming, potentially exacerbating chronic pain and risk of injury.

# Chapter 2

## *Want to improve speed and acceleration?*

## *Train like a Bobsledder?*

Aside from skill, one major factor of field sport success is separation within the first 5-10 yards. This comes from the ability to rapidly accelerate, decelerate, and change direction. Think Barry Sanders or Tyreek Hill on the football field, Messi on the soccer field, Westbrook on the basketball court, Nadal on the tennis court, et. Looking at the 15m sprint combine scoring for the USA Bobsled team, a sub 2.20 15m sprint (men) and 2.33 15m sprint (women) certainly meets that criteria.

Bobsledders must generate enough force to accelerate a 384 pound empty 2-man sled or 462 pound 4-man sled 50 meters in roughly 5 seconds! That takes a combination of significant strength, power, and speed to move a sled that heavy that fast. An athlete able to attain and then maintain these force-production qualities would be dangerous on any field of play.

> **Force = Mass*Acceleration**
>
> If you have a glass window 40 feet away, throw a shot-put at it and it may not even reach; Throw a Whiffle ball as fast as you can and it surely bounces back off the glass; however, a baseball is the right balance of mass and speed to shatter it.

A 2014 article looking at the preparation of Bobsledders for the Sochi Olympics expressed that the athletes not only need to be big enough to create enough momentum while sliding down the track, but they also need to create enough force in a short period of time to reach push speeds of roughly 25mph (12).

Similar physical characteristics to some of the best defensive lineman, linebackers, running backs, and tight ends in the National Football League.

A 1996 study out of the *Journal of Strength and Conditioning Research* looked at the vertical jumps, 2-arm underhand shot tosses, 30m sprint, 100m sprint, 5 consecutive hop test, and 30 second Wingate test, of 22 National Championships push competitors. **The athletes who performed the best in the push also had the best vertical jumps and 30m sprints** (21).

To get a better picture, let us look at the combine and testing protocols for the *Canadian* and *USA Bobsled Teams*.

### Bobsleigh CANADA Skeleton National Bobsleigh Program Athletic Testing Protocols

- 60m Sprint
- 1080 Sprint: The 1080 Sprint is a test utilizing a mechanism which allows evaluation of the Athlete's force production during a sprint test over 40m (distance subject to change by the tester), at speed, against constant external loads 5, 10, and 15kg. (*This is a top of the line $19,300.00 testing device: 1080 Sprint*)
- Standing Long Jump
- Power Clean: 1 Rep Max
- Front Squat: 3 Rep Max

Looking at the performance scoring chart example given on their team site a power clean of 160kg (352lbs) nets an athlete

26

96 points, while a power clean of 130kg (286lbs) netted a separate athlete 82 points.

When it comes to the standing broad jump, a jump of 3.22m (10'6") netted 93 points, while 3.01m (9'10 ½ ") netted a separate athlete 85 points. While a 2.07s fifteen-meter sprint earned 98 points, while a 2.14s sprint earned 91 points. When extending the sprint out to 30m, 3.65s earned 90 points, while 3.78s earned 77 points.

In the past we have enjoyed success with these types of point systems as they provide a weighted look at the overall development of each player on top of the teams over time. Keeping **things relative to the needs of the sport and athlete** is always key in allowing it to have a direct impact on competitive performance in sport.

> *"Everyone is a genius. But if you judge a fish by its ability to climb a tree, it will live its whole life believing that it is stupid."*
> — Albert Einstein

Keeping in mind specific and measurable differences that apply to the individual position groups in team sports can make a big difference. For example, a soccer goalie has little in common with a midfielder, while an offensive lineman in football has little in common with the team's defensive backs.

Looking at the US Team's testing combine;

- Times for 0-15, 0-30, 0-45, and 15-45 (30m split).
- Standing Broad Jump
- Underhand forward shot toss: Men will throw a 16lb shot. Women will throw a 12lb shot
- National Team Camp: 1 rep power clean and 3 rep back squat

Here is a sampling of the scoring. For both the men's and women's full charts check out the USA team's combine page.

15m Sprint:

| Men | Women |
|---|---|
| 2.05s = 100 points | 2.20s = 100 points |
| 2.12s = 90 points | 2.27s = 90 points |
| 2.18s = 80 points | 2.33s = 80 points |
| 2.25s = 70 points | 2.40s = 70 points |

30m Sprint:

| Men | Women |
|---|---|
| 3.55s = 100 points | 3.85s = 100 points |
| 3.68s = 90 points | 3.98s = 90 points |
| 3.81s = 80 points | 4.11s = 80 points |
| 3.94s = 70 points | 4.24s = 70 points |

## 45m sprint:

| Men | Women |
|---|---|
| 5.10s = 100 points | 5.60s = 100 points |
| 5.26s = 90 points | 5.76s = 90 points |
| 5.42s = 80 points | 5.92s = 80 points |
| 5.58s = 70 points | 6.08s = 70 points |

## Broad Jump:

| Men | Women |
|---|---|
| 3.35m = 100 points | 3.00m = 100 points |
| 3.16m = 90 points | 2.81m = 90 points |
| 2.97m = 80 points | 2.62m = 80 points |
| 2.78m = 70 points | 2.43m = 70 points |

## Power Clean

| Men | Women |
|---|---|
| 150kg = 100 points | 100kg = 100 points |
| 130kg = 90 points | 87.5kg = 90 points |
| 110kg = 80 points | 75.0kg = 80 points |
| 90.0kg = 70 points | 62.5kg = 70 points |

Back Squat

| Men | Women |
|-----|-------|
| **Men** | **Women** |
| 200kg = 100 points | 130kg = 100 points |
| 175kg = 90 points | 105kg = 90 points |
| 150kg = 80 points | 80.0kg = 80 points |
| 125kg = 70 points | 62.5kg = 70 points |

A paper out of the *Russian State University of Physical Culture, Sport, Youth, and Tourism* looked at the yearlong training load for competitive bobsledders. The paper included a chart comparing the size, strength, speed, and power difference of bobsledders in 1990 vs 2010 [14].

Average assessment of male bobsledders in 1990 and 2010.

| Year | Weight | Back Sq | Front Sq | St Tri Ju | 30m(flying) |
|------|--------|---------|----------|-----------|-------------|
| 1990 | 89.1kg | 176.77kg | 124.84kg | 9.07m | 3.0s |
| 2010 | 97.6kg | 182.73kg | 117.7kg | 8.91m | 3.15 |

From looking at the Canadian and USA team's testing numbers (and the above study), these athletes weigh over 200lbs, both the men's and women's teams Power clean between 110-160kg (242-352lbs) and 75-100kg (165-220lbs), Squat over 150kg (330lbs) and 80kg (165lbs), broad jump nearly 10 feet, and run a 30m sprint in sub 4.0 and 4.25 seconds, respectively. *Would these numbers get some of these girls or guys noticed at an NFL Combine?*

How does all this testing tie into their overall athletic ability?

## Jumping Ability

Power output in both loaded and unloaded jumps has been linked to an athlete's ability to accelerate. The start of a sprint off the blocks on a track, get out of a cut to change direction and create a breakaway play, or drive a bobsled fast enough to take Olympic gold. 2014 research on youth soccer players, found **significant positive correlations between relative strength, jumping ability, and 20m sprint performance** (7).

A study on Rugby players had similar findings; **the players with the best jump height and power output in the drop jump, countermovement jump, and 35kg squat jump, also had the best 5, 10, and 30m sprint times** (10). A study from 2014 had similar findings, they found that **the soccer players who could generate the most force in the countermovement jump, also had the best sprint acceleration** (20).

## Power Clean, anyone?

According to a 2017 paper out of East Tennessee State University, *"in the 2014 PPC, the 1RM Power Clean was the single most predictive variable of pushing performance among TOP 10*

31

*athletes and was the only one to reach statistical significance* (15)."

In 2008 researchers looked to see if performance in the hang power clean correlated to jumping, 20-meter sprint, and 5-5 change of direction in 29 Australian Rules football players. The researchers found significant correlations, **the athletes who performed the best in the power clean (relative to their bodyweight) also had performed** better in 20-meter sprint performance, maximum strength, and jumping tests.

> The same strength and power qualities needed to be successful in the hang power clean, were the same qualities required for better performance in short sprint acceleration and jumping abilities (18).

In a 2004 study, researchers compared the effects of Olympic lifting and conventional power lifting on field performance tests including agility (T drill), vertical jump, and 40-yard sprint in college football players.

They found that after 15 weeks of 4 day a week training, **the Olympic lifting group saw an 18% better improvement in the 1RM squat, nearly 2 times greater improvement in the 40-yard sprint than the traditional powerlifting group**. Of significance, were the vertical jump gains. **The O-lift group saw a 6.8cm gain in jump height while the traditional power lifting group saw a 0.5cm gain** (17).

32

## Resisted sprinting and sled pushing?

A 2018 meta-analysis of 13 studies found **resisted sprint training to be an effective method for improving acceleration** (1). A separate review study from the 2016 *Sports Medicine* journal found speed could be improved when **loads of 30% body mass or less were used in resisted sprints** (23).

One systematic review looked at the effect different sprint training methods had on sprint performance and found **resisted sprinting to be at or near the top when it came to improving short sprints and acceleration** (28).

One idea might be to tap into Postactivation Potentiation and utilize both squats and resisted sprints. In 2019, researchers found that **squats at 80% combined with resisted sprints at 12.5% BM were more effective at improving 30m sprint, countermovement jump, and change of direction, than resisted sprinting or squatting by themselves** (22). *(For much more on Postactivation Potentiation check out chapter 3.)*

## How much resistance in resisted sprints and sled pushes?

### Sled Push Studies

A recent study from the *Scandinavian Journal of Medicine and Science in Sports* recruited 50 high school athletes to figure out which sled resistances led to better improvements in sprint and vertical jump after 8 weeks of training. They assigned the athletes to one of 4 groups: control, light resistance, moderate resistance, and heavy resistance. Light resistance led to a 25% decrease in speed, moderate a 50% decrease, and heavy a 75% decrease and tested vert, sprint, hex bar deadlift, and standing long jump.

The Light group did 22.5m (meters) per sprint for a total of 270-405m per workout. Meanwhile, the Moderate group did 15m per sprint for a total of 180-270m per workout. The Heavy group did 7.5m per sprint and 90-135m total per workout. All workouts had 3 minutes of rest between sprints (5).

Here are the before and after results for vert and sprint (5):

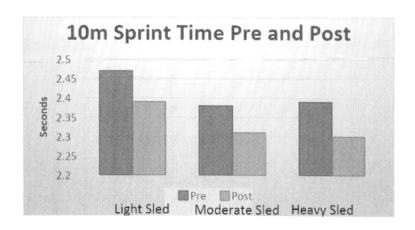

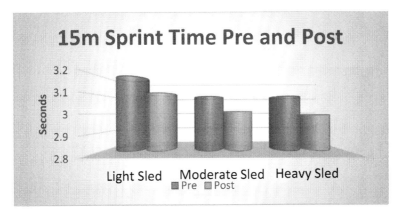

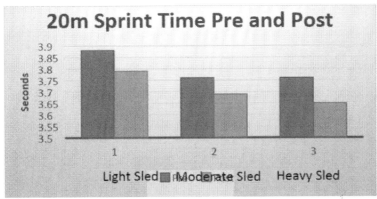

Resisted sled pushes at different loads may positively impact sprinting performance after 8 weeks of training. **Now, what is the optimal load?**

Using something called Vdec, basically the decrease in maximal velocity, the same research team (but in a separate 2020 study (6)) was able to determine optimal load for 3 different strength qualities:

- **Speed strength** = roughly 0-40%BM

35

- **Power** = roughly 40-80%BM

- **Strength Speed** = roughly 80% plus

According to the researchers *"adopting the Vdec method will allow practitioners to identify different training zones during resisted sled pushing, such as speed-strength, power, and strength-speed. Matching the training zone to the athlete's force-velocity characteristic could potentially yield better training results than simply applying the same resistive load for all athletes (5)."*

Compared to the one size fits all sled push approach, this Vdec individualized resistance approach to sled pushing allows for both stronger and weaker athletes to optimize specific strength qualities.

Resisted Sprint Study

In a similar study, this one on Rugby and Lacrosse players, researchers used the same methods to determine optimal resisted sprint loads.

The researchers found the average resistance sprint loads that corresponded to a Vdec were:

- 25% Vdec = 33% BM (**Speed Strength**)
- 50% Vdec = 66% BM (**Power**)
- 75% Vdec = 100% BM (**Strength Speed**)

The study authors expressed that heavier sled pulls were a form of horizontal resistance training, to be included and periodized throughout the overall strength and conditioning program.

As in the sled push study, the researchers found three different training zones (*speed strength, power, strength speed*) that can be used to optimize sled loads based on training goals throughout the season (4).

One other study, this one from the 2018 *European Journal of Applied Physiology*, found a Vdec of 50% in loads ranging from **69-96% BM** (9).

> **Don't trade your barbell in for a sled just yet!**
>
> A 2016 study found:
>
> sets of 4-8 reps @ 40-60% of 1RM in the deep back squat was more effective than multiple sets of 20m resisted sprints at 12.6% BM for improving 20 and 50m sprint performance (11)

Postactivation Potentiation (PAP):

Lifting something heavy or performing an explosive power movement prior to an unloaded sprint, jump or biomechanically similar movement, can potentiate/augment the performance/force generated in the successive movement.

> In a 2005 paper, researcher Daniel Robbins defines postactivation potentiation (PAP) as *"a phenomenon by which the force exerted by a muscle is increased due to its previous contraction (24)"*, whereby previous contraction of a muscle can influence the performance of subsequent contractions.

An example of this is a set of 3Rep Max back squats, rest, then run a 20 meter sprint. A second example is a 3RM Hex Bar deadlift, rest, then perform an unloaded countermovement jump.

Two recent Meta-analyses of dozens of studies, found the overall results of the literature to point toward the effectiveness of both complex and contrast training as methods to induce PAP for augmentation of subsequent performances in short sprints and jumping (8, 2).

In fact, a 2010 study out of the *University of Hawaii* found an **decrease of 0.04-0.34 seconds in the 100m sprint when recreationally trained women did a set 4RM back squats prior to 100m sprint test** (19).

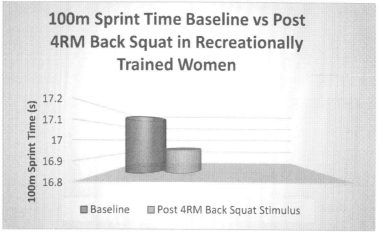

Another study, this one out of the *Sport and Exercise Science Research Center at Swansea University* looked at the PAP effect 3 reps at 90%(1RM) had on 5 and 10m sprint times in a group of professional Rugby players (3). The study method breakdown was:

- Complete baseline 10m sprint with 5m split

- Active rest 20 minutes

- Complete 1 set of 3 reps in the back squat at 91% of 1RM

- Perform 10m sprint (with 5m split time) at 4, 8, 12, and 16 minutes post squat stimulus.

*47% of athletes hit their best 5m split time at 8 minutes post 3 rep squat set, while 53.3% did their best in the 10m sprint with the same rest.*

Taking the Postactivation Potentiation phenomenon to the next level, French sport scientist Gilles Cometti created something called the ***French Contrast Method***. *Check out chapter 3 for more on this.*

## Front Squat vs Back Squat

A 2015 study looked at the EMG activity differences of front and back squat using heavy loads. On two separate testing sessions, one for front and one for back, the subjects worked their way up to their one rep max while the researchers tested which muscles are most active in both squats. Here is what the researchers found (30):

During the **Front Squat:**

- The Rectus Femoris (RF) was roughly **25%** more active

- The <u>Vastus Medialis (VMO)</u> was **13.5%** more active
- The <u>Vastus Lateralis (VL)</u> was roughly **8%** more active
- The <u>Erector Spinae (ES)</u> was nearly **7%** more active

During the **Back Squat:**

- The <u>Biceps Femoris (BF)</u> was roughly **8%** more active
- The <u>Semitendinosus (ST)</u> was nearly **35%** more active

While the activation levels for the <u>Glute Max (GM)</u> was roughly the same in both squats!

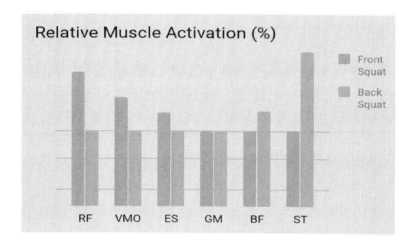

The study also looked at the muscle activity during both the concentric and eccentric phases of the max rep for each squat. Below are a few of the more significant findings:

During the Front Squat:

- The <u>Vastus Medialis</u> was nearly **11% more active during the concentric phase** vs the eccentric phase.
- The <u>Vastus Lateralis</u> was roughly **17% more active during the concentric phase** vs eccentric phase.
- The <u>Glute Max</u> was also **55% more active during the concentric phase** vs the eccentric phase.
- <u>Biceps Femoris</u> nearly **50% more active in the concentric phase** vs eccentric phase.

During the Back Squat:

- The <u>Glute Max</u> was **64.24% more active during the concentric phase** vs eccentric phase.
- The <u>Biceps Femoris</u> was nearly **87% more active in the concentric phase** vs eccentric phase
- Lastly, the <u>Semitendinosus</u> was roughly **93% more active in the concentric phase** vs eccentric phase

From looking at the study results, as well as the results of a 2008 study from the *Journal of Strength and Conditioning Research, do* **front squats may have a greater impact on change of direction, while back squats may be better for improving linear speed and acceleration?**

In the 2008 study, researchers looked at the correlation between front squat, power clean, linear speed, and change of direction. The researchers found that **the athletes who front squatted more *(avg 230lbs vs 212lbs)* and power cleaned more** *(avg 176lbs vs 154lbs)*, **performed better in the 5-5 change of direction eval** (18).

**Bar Speed:**

For safety (*and improving explosiveness*) purposes, concentric bar speeds of 1 to 1.5 meters per second in squatting and pressing movements can be effective. Feel free to add a pause at the bottom to work on true muscular strength (*without the help of elastic energy*) by minimizing stretch reflex.

Developing strength and speed is always the key to most performance goals. While many interpretations have been presented in different coaching circles, the general rules of the strength - speed continuum with regards to velocity is:

| Adaptation: | Absolute Strength | Strength - Speed | Power | Speed - Strength | Explosive Speed |
|---|---|---|---|---|---|
| Speed (m/s) | <.5 | .5 - .75 | .75 - 1.0 | 1.0 - 1.3 | > 1.3 |

Oftentimes, an experienced coach may be more beneficial than an arbitrary velocity recommendation from a book. With that in mind, this chart can be useful when interpreting training status and the adaptations you are looking for. General Adaptation Syndrome (GAS) suggests that an athlete adapts to the stress places on them – slow stress means a slow athlete, over time.

42

**Bar Speed Devices:**

- Kinetic Performance's Gymaware
- Assess to Perform Bar Sensei
- Push Strength Push Band
- Iron Path App


## The Age-Old Debate of Squat Depth and the "Bad Knees":

### Questions answered by this meta-analysis:

Hartmann H, Wirth K, Klusemann M. **Analysis of the load on the knee joint and vertebral column with changes in depth and weight load.** *Journal of Sports Medicine.* 43; Pp 993-1008. 2013.

**Why squats to parallel can be bad for the knees:** *"Based on biomechanical calculations and measurements of cadaver knee joints, the highest retropatellar compressive forces and greatest compressive stresses are observed at 90 degrees". In other words, if you stop the lowering phase and transition to the concentric phase at 90-degree knee bend, you are exposing your knees to the greatest compressive stresses (16)"*

**Why deep squats are good for the knees:** *"With increasing flexion, the additional contact between the quadriceps tendon and the intercondylar notch as the tendofemoral support surface (wrapping effect) contribute to an enhanced load distribution and enhanced force transfer. Because lower weights are used in the deep back squat and regular strength training practice leads to* functional adaptations of passive tissue, concerns about degenerative changes of the tendofemoral complex are unfounded and unproven (16)."

**Why squats to parallel can be bad for women:** *"Women need to be particularly careful during half and parallel squat as female cadaver knees have been shown to possess 33% lower contact areas of the patellofemoral joint than male samples at 120 and 90-degree knee flexion (16)."*

**More on why parallel squats can be bad for the knees:** *"The execution of a half squat cannot be recommended because the turning point is initiated in a knee joint angle amplitude, where the highest patellofemoral compressive forces and greatest compressive stresses occur with only a minor tendofemoral support surface (16)."*

**Why parallel squats can be bad for the low back:** *"The restriction of the forward knee placement will result in changes to the knee hip coordination with greater forward leaning and ventral flexion of the thoracic and lumbar spine. This evasive movement elicits greater anterior shear forces on intervertebral discs and causes tensile forces on intervertebral ligaments. For that reason, instructions about a restriction of the forward knee displacement must be strictly avoided. This recommendation is based on a misinterpretation of existing data and should be removed in future practical literature (16)."*

**Why you should deep squat with a controlled eccentric tempo:** *"The higher the lowering speed in the descent phase, the higher the developing deceleration phase to avoid a dipping movement and hence a rising increase of tibiofemoral shear and compressive forces in the turning point of the squat. For that reason, care should be taken to complete a slow and controlled execution comprising a descent phase of 3 to 4 seconds in the deep squat corresponding to an average angular velocity in the knee joint of 46.66 and 35 degrees/sec respectively (16)."*

**Another reason parallel squats may be bad for women:** *"Females possess significant lower compressive strength of vertebral bodies because of their significantly lower end plate cross sectional area than their male counterparts. This means that the female lumbar vertebral is exposed to higher axial compressive stress than a male spine when subjected to equivalent load (16)."*

**And finally! why deep squats may be better for your ACL:** *"In the* deep squat loads of 1.16- and 2.27-times body weight accounted for 11.62% and 28.9% *of the tensile strength of an ACL in 16 to 35 year olds. The calculated anterior shear forces in the* half squat with a load of 1.16 times bodyweight accounts for between 33.29 and 41.56%. *Based on these calculations, in deep squats, neither* *posterior nor anterior shear forces may reach magnitudes that could harm an intact PCL or ACL (16)."*

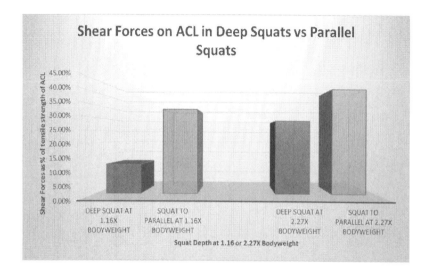

### Broad Jump vs Vertical Jump:

A 1987 study from the *Canadian Journal of Sport Sciences* looked at the different contributions of the muscles about the hips, knees, and ankles in the standing broad vs vertical jump.

The researchers found greater contributions from the hips and ankles in the broad jump, while the knees were more active in the vertical jump. Below are some of the findings (25):

Broad Jump vs Vertical Jump: Hip, Knee, and Ankle Activity

### Training in the Sand

Did you know that **training in the sand can lead to 3X greater improvements in speed and agility** than training on solid surfaces?

From *Make a Muscle: Sand as an Effective Training Tool in Gatehouse Media* (27):

*"A study published in the Sports Medicine and Doping Studies Journal tested two groups of athletes in two separate agility tests, the T Drill Agility test and the 505 agility drill. Each group was then taken through 10 weeks of three times per week training. The only differences in training were **one group performed all of the training exercises on solid surface while the other group performed the exercises on sand.***

*After 10 weeks of training, the hard training surface improved their T test time from 15.1 seconds on average to 14.4 seconds on average, for a .7-second improvement. The sand training group significantly improved their T test time from 15.3 seconds to 13.2 seconds for a 2.1-second improvement. That is nearly a 14 percent improvement in agility over a 10-week time period. The sand training group also made significant improvements in the 505 agility test, while the hard training surface group's results were minimal.*

*In a 1982 Sports Illustrated article, NFL great Walter Payton was asked about his off-season training, which included a high volume of sand training workouts. Payton believed it was the constant adjustments required for successful sprinting and cutting in the sand that were major contributors to his speed, agility, and low rate of injury. Researchers believe the sand increases the neuromuscular demand on the body. The instability of the surface creates repeated losses of balance, which in turn forces the stabilizer muscles throughout our body to work synergistically in order to maintain balance.*

*Countless professional athletes have followed Payton. Year after year, athletes from NFL, NBA and NHL all-stars to Olympic hopefuls and college stars make their way out to Manhattan Beach California for off-season workouts at the famous sand Dune Park. Division I college football teams, including Michigan, Oregon, Ohio State, Miami, Penn State and Georgia Southern, have all installed sandpits to enhance the speed, agility, and overall athleticism of their athletes. Some high-performance strength and conditioning centers and CrossFit boxes have also begun utilizing sandpit training.*

*These athletes and coaches realize the significant benefits sand training can have on speed, jumping ability and overall condition. Sprinting in the sand leads to an increased demand of the hamstrings as extensors of the hips. During the drive phase, the feet sink and slide in the sand, similar to tires spinning in mud. This in turn increases the mechanical work of the hamstrings. Jumping in the sand is similar and can lead to significant improvements in jumping ability.*

*A study from the Journal of Sports Medicine had two groups of athletes train three times per week for four weeks. One group trained on sand while the other trained on grass. The group that trained on the sand saw significantly greater improvements in their squat jump compared to the grass-training group. Not only did the group training on the sand see better athletic gains, but they also incurred less muscle damage in the process.*

*In 2003, a research team out of Japan set out to determine the differences in muscle breakdown and soreness between jumping in the sand and jumping on solid ground. The researchers found significantly less muscle breakdown and associated soreness when jumping on the sand.*

*Training in the sand is also a great way for decreasing the risk of injury in the lower extremities. For example, the instability of the sand increases the demand on the small muscles that stabilize the ankle. This in turn strengthens those muscles, leading to a more stable joint. The same results can be seen in the knee and hip joints when training on the sand. It is for these reasons that some doctors and physiotherapists recommend their patients to incorporate sand walking or jogging into the final stages of their recovery."*

For more benefits, training ideas, programs, and a sand exercise library, be sure to pick up book # 2 in the **_Specific Sports Training and Athletic Workout Programs_ series**, Sand Training For Sports: A Guide to the Science of sand training and sand based workout routines for athletes.

**Don't have sand readily available?** A simple walk through the woods or state park can be a great option. From the *Journal of Experimental Biology*, a 2013 study indicated major changes in muscle activation patterns while walking on uneven surfaces (31). Although this was a small study of only 11 participants, the results seemed to favor increased co-activation / co-contraction and/or *"mutual muscle contraction"* between the major muscles of the leg.

This study's findings could provide valuable information for both injury prevention and athletic performance. The variability of uneven surfaces causes changes in step length and distances. This alters the dynamic from simple walking to a now low-end reactive drill that increases the mechanical work on the tissue. This enhances low-end CNS activity by causing cooperative and stabilizing interactions between the active muscles.

*"Walking on the uneven terrain resulted in a significant increase in energy expenditure compared with the other surfaces. Net **metabolic rate increased by approximately 28%***

*Work performed by the ankle over a stride did not change appreciably on the uneven surface, but **the hip performed 62% more positive work and the knee 26% more negative work***" (31).

The reactivity of simply walking on a variable surface is stimulating to CNS in that every step taken is a slightly different. The way the ankles, knees, hips, trunk, and arms take on flexion, extension and rotation are based on input from and negotiation with the ground each step. INTRA-step variability brings different amounts of flexion at the knees, hips, and trunk, accompanied by all the different torques and force vectors brought on by gravity and momentum.

One often-overlooked benefit to walking on uneven surfaces is that it can address the often-times under-developed musculature of the hips, groin / adductors, and hamstrings. Not only can this potentially lead to improved performance and recovery, but it can also lead to a decreased risk of injury.

A study done on elderly subjects found a significant increase in balance-control in subjects participating in a perturbation-based training *(where a force is applied to disturb balance)* program. While elderly subjects may not the best example of athletic prowess, this shows how late in life even an 8-week training program can still benefit you. With regards to *"elderly performance"*, we see that roughly 60% of falls are due to *"extrinsic factors"* like slips, trips, or falling from stairs, all of which can result from uneven surfaces and/or perturbed walking (32).

While taking a gentle stroll through the woods may not increase explosive abilities directly, it may act as a **low-level neuromuscular recovery and restoration** option. This can make it an increasingly valuable piece of any training program *(and the best part is that it's free and accessible)*.

# Chapter 3

## *Postactivation Potentiation*

Is there a method of training in which individuals can make immediate gains in vertical jump, acceleration, and agility?

In 2005, in his paper **Postactivation potentiation and its practical applicability: a brief review,** Robbins defined postactivation potentiation (PAP) as *"a phenomenon by which the force exerted by a muscle is increased due to its previous contraction (43)",* wherein, the contractile history of a muscle influences the mechanical performance of subsequent muscle contractions.

Similar training methods were reportedly used by Eastern Bloc Olympic training coaches back in the 1980's. In a 1996 study, Schmidtleicher and Gullich explained the effects this type of training can have on immediate Maximal-Voluntary Contraction (MVC):

*"The short-term MVC-effects can be used to improve performance during competition by integrating the MVCs into the warm-up pro-gramme. Furthermore, athletes can profit from the effect of MVCs in training, too. If. during specific speed-strength training, maximum performances are achieved under conditions of improved neuromuscular activation (after MVCs], particularly high adaptations are to be expected (23)"*

*"The potentiation of neuromuscular activation and explosive force is characterized by a high interindividual variability of the time course. It must be concluded that, in order*

*to guarantee the highest possible effectiveness, it is necessary to determine individually the optimal interval be-tween treatment MVCs and the subsequent speed-strength performances (23)."*

In other words, a max voluntary contraction prior to a contrasting explosive speed-based exercise (jumps, throws, bounds, skips, etc).

**Does this method really work?** Can trainees improve sprint and jumping performance within a matter of minutes? Let us look at what the research on PAP has to say?

As we saw in chapter 2, two meta-analyses of dozens of studies, found the overall results of the literature to point toward the effectiveness of both complex and contrast training as methods to induce PAP for augmentation of subsequent performances in short sprints and jumping (12,4).

## What are some that factors affect the PAP response?

A 2016 paper found vertical jump potentiation was dependent upon several individual characteristics including:

- o Training background
- o Neuromuscular characteristics
- o Relative strength
- o Preceding exercise
- o Rest interval
- o Current fatigue state

- Volume-load completed

## The Impact that Warm-Up and Prior activity has on subsequent performance.

Research from 2014 on *Rugby Union* players (13) found that **morning weight training led to better performance in the 40m sprint, countermovement jump, bench press, and squat testing later in the day**. For the morning sessions, at 9:00am, the athletes separated into 3 groups: One group did 5 x 40-meter sprints, a second group did a weight training workout consisting of 12 x 3 reps in the squat and bench press, and the last group was the rested control group.

The afternoon testing took place six hours later at 3:00pm. Each athlete had their salivary testosterone levels measured, followed by testing in the 3RM bench press, 3RM squat, countermovement vertical jump, and a 40-meter sprint evaluation.

**The morning weight training group saw a significantly greater afternoon performance than the rested control group, and still moderately better testing performance than the sprinting session group**. The following is a comparison of weights vs control (13):

| Evaluation | AM Strength Training | AM Control (rested) |
|---|---|---|
| 40m Sprint | 5.16s | 5.23s |
| CMJ Power | 4292(W) | 4408(W) |
| 3RM Squat | 168.0 kg | 175.0 kg |
| 3RM Bench Press | 139.0 kg | 144.0 kg |

Other studies have shown similar effects (10,39,50), including one out of the *University of North Carolina*. In this 2013 study researchers found that **working out with weights 4-6 hours prior led to improvements in overhead backward shot throw performance** (18).

**One interesting study on Hockey players found that having** the athletes work out using **contrast training methods six hours prior** not only led to improvements in the broad as well as the countermovement jumps, but **also improved on-ice 40m conditioning sprint performance** (31).

> **Is the Overhead Medicine ball throw a valid predictor of explosive power?**
>
> In a 2001 study out of the *Journal of Strength and Conditioning Research*, subjects did an overhead med ball throw followed by a countermovement vertical jump. The researchers found a positive correlation between the distance the subjects were able to overhead throw and power in the jump test (47).

## The Contrast workout was 5 sets of:

**A1:** Inertia Back Squat X 5 reps with 85%1RM at 4X01 tempo

**A2:** Squat Jumps x 6

Six hours after the Contrast Training session researchers saw the **broad jump improve from 254.1(cm) to 266.3 (cm) (12.2cm total!),** while **total sprint time decreased from 56.2 to 53.1 seconds**, and the **mean sprint speed increased from 6.4(m/s) to 6.8(m/s).**

**These studies show that working out at least 6 hours prior to an afternoon session may increase testosterone, increase vertical and broad jump, and increase speed.**

**Are there any specific warm-ups we can do to improve explosiveness during a workout?**

Research out of the *School of Physiotherapy in Melbourne Australia* enlisted 22 elite Australian Rules Football players to test the effects of three different warm-up protocols on jump performance. **The group that did the low load glute specific warm up exercises saw significantly greater power output numbers than the control and vibration warm up groups** (14).

Warming up the nervous system between 4-6 hours prior and waking up the hip extensors with light load training directly prior seems to positively impact explosiveness and testing performance. Listening to industry leader James Radcliffe, University of Oregon Strength and Speed coach speak on game day workouts shed light even on the idea of a light fast-explosive training complex early on game day.

A specific routine that we have used early in a day before an afternoon game for football athletes (can be used with others!) looks like this: "Game-Day 50" – 5 moves x 10 Reps of each movement, repeated 2-4 times (empty barbell for speed and to avoid any fatigue):

A1 – BB Hang Clean Pull / Jump Shrug

A2 – BB Snatch Pull / Jump Shrug

A3 – BB Front Squat (mobility focus)

A4 – BB Push Press or Split Jerk (explosive focus)

A5 – BB Jump Squat

This routine is meant to be done without putting the barbell down, reinstalling existing motor-patterns at a low-fatigue but high activation rate. Only used with more advanced athletes with sufficient training experience in these exercises (*trying to minimize shock to the body for CNS-fatigue purposes*)

One major factor that may affect PAP (as well as all other training variables and programs used with an athlete) is **Training experience and strength levels.**

**Postactivation response and training experience:**

A 2013 meta-analysis of 32 studies on postactivation potentiation found that (55):

- **Experienced athletes responded better than untrained individuals**
- Multiple sets were more effective than single sets. **Untrained individuals had 104% greater power augmentation with multiple sets** vs single sets, while **experienced athletes saw their power augment as much as 320%** while performing multiple sets vs single sets.
- **Rest periods of 3-7 and 7-10 minutes** elicited the greatest augmentation responses for experienced and trained athletes.

In line with these findings on experienced athletes, a 2003 study also found a significantly greater postactivation power increase in the experienced athlete group versus the less experienced recreational group (11).

**Do Strength Levels Affect PAP Variables?**

Research from 2010 found that **stronger athletes may need shorter rest periods** after a strength PAP stimulus exercise, while

**weaker athletes may need longer rest periods.** For stronger athletes, the researchers found **5-10 minute** rest ranges were optimal, while **15-20 minutes** worked best for the weaker athletes (29).

At *Edith Cowen University,* researchers recruited *French Rugby League* players to determine if the strength level of the athletes played a role in the rest period length needed for postacitvation augmentation. Stronger rugby players squatted over 2X bodyweight, while weaker players squatted 1.5-2X bodyweight.

After a thorough warm-up, the athletes took part in the baseline assessment of 3 sets of 1 in the unloaded squat jump. The Rugby players then rested 10 minutes. At the 10 minute mark they performed a set of 3 back squats at 90% 1RM. To test the PAP augmentation response, they then did max effort single rep unloaded jump squats at 15s, 3min, 6min, 9min, and 12 mins post back squat set.

The **>2X bodyweight squat group saw increases** in power and

> **Jump Training for Explosiveness – Tip #1:**
>
> While jumping helps increase the rate of muscle contraction and explosiveness, **it can be a lot impact on the joints, if that is not the goal try standard box jumps to eliminate the downward force on landings –** installing an upright or straight leg landing helps get rid of the deep squat on the box and improves true vertical jumping!

jump height at 3, 6, 9, and 12, with a **peak at 6 minutes**, while the **1.5-2X bodyweight squat group saw a rise** in power and jump height **at 6 and 9 minutes**. Both groups saw **decreases in power at 15s post squat set.**

Continuing with the factors that can affect PAP let us look at research exploring **Rest Duration for Jumping and Running Performance.**

As mentioned earlier in the 2007 research out of the *Department of Sports Science at the University of Wales* looked at the impacts different rest periods had on the postactivation potentiation response in twenty three professional rugby players.

**For the lower body segment of the study, the athletes:**

- **Set a baseline** power output in their countermovement jump
- **Rested 10 minutes**
- Then did a **set of 3RM back squats.**
- At 15s, 4min, 8min, 12min, 16min, and 20min post 3RM squat the athletes **performed one countermovement jump test.**

On average, **athlete power dropped below baseline with 15s or rest, but increased to its peak at 8 and 12 minutes post squat set** (15).

Researchers from the *Sport and Exercise Science Research Center at Swansea University* looked at the effect 3 reps at 90%(1RM) in the back squat had on 5 and 10m sprint times in a group of professional Rugby players (5).

> **The breakdown of the study method was:**
> - Complete **baseline 10m sprint** with 5m split
> - Active **rest 20 minutes**
> - **1 set of 3 rep back squat at 91%** (1RM)
> - **Perform 10m sprint** (with 5m split time) at 4, 8, 12, and 16 minutes post squat stimulus.

From looking at these studies, the rest period, as determined by individual differences and exercise selection, seems to play an important role in potentiation outcomes.


### Exercise Selection

Which is better, **jumping/plyo or weight training**, as a postactivation potentiation stimulus? A research team out of the *Human Performance Laboratory at Cal State Fullerton* set out to answer this question. They had 12 in season track and field athletes go through two testing protocols (53):

**1st Protocol:** Seven consecutive squat jumps, rest 3 mins, then 5 reps of back squat at 85%, rest 3 mins, then another set of 7 consecutive squat jumps.

**2nd Protocol:** Seven consecutive squat jumps, rest 3 mins, 5 consecutive squat jumps, rest 3 mins, then another set of 7 consecutive squat jumps.

The 5 rep back squat at 85% led to a significant improvement in jump height, while the 5 consecutive unloaded jump squats led to a decrease in jump height.

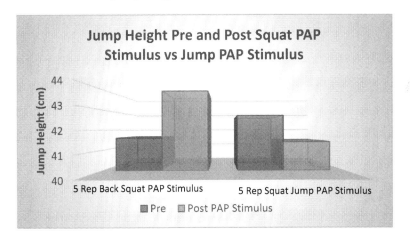

The results of this study showed that **weight training can be more effective at eliciting a positive vertical jump PAP response than <u>unloaded</u> jumping.** What happens if an athlete adds some resistance to the stimulus jumping exercise?

A 2015 study looked at the effects loaded bounding drills used as a conditioning stimulus had on 10m and 20m sprint performance. After baseline testing the subjects either went for a walk, performed a set of bodyweight only alternate leg bounding, or performed a set of weight vest loaded (*at 10% of body mass*) alternate leg bounding (51).

The loaded weight vest stimulus led to greater improvements in both 10 and 20m sprint speed (51). Pointing us back to the value of resistance training in performance-enhancement training – again we can likely credit this to the higher levels of

> **Jump Training for Explosiveness – Tip #2:**
>
> 2 leg jumps are good, but great athletes are forced to produce big forces often on only 1 leg, **try a staggered "stride-stance" really driving off the front leg** to challenge single leg and first-step explosiveness.

voluntary speed of muscular contraction, similar to how the 85% squatting or MVC work elicits PAP, but on the speed end of the spectrum.

Another study, this one on Rugby Union players, found that loading a bar at 20-60% in hex bar or bar across the back/shoulders jump squats, increased peak power and vertical jump height (49).

**Can unloaded plyometric/jumping play a role in augmenting subsequent performance?** To test this, researchers had eight national-level decathletes perform 6 long-jump attempts separated by 10-min recoveries.

The experimental condition performed 3 rebound vertical jumps as conditioning stimulus 3 minutes prior to the final five attempts, while the control condition rested.

**The experimental condition (*vertical jumps prior*), saw their long jump performance improve, ranging from 5.95m on first attempt to roughly 6.2m on their 5th and 6th attempts**.

The control condition saw their performances deteriorate, averaging roughly 6.05m on first attempt, then dropping to 5.96 on the third attempt, and finishing just below 6.0m on the final attempt (6).

A separate study looked at the impact plyometrics and specific jump-training had on several on-field performance markers including change of direction, acceleration, and subsequent jumping performance. In this study the researchers had athletes perform accentuated drop jumps prior to testing countermovement jumps, squat jumps, 10m sprints, 30m sprints, and change of direction (8).

> **Jump Training for Explosiveness – Tip #3:**
>
> After mastering the stride-stance box jump, try applying more specific agility components, doing a **"Power" jump off and away from the front leg** to mimic and improve your explosive cutting ability

This study found **minimal change in 10 and 30m straight sprint times with the drop jump stimulus, but they did find a significant improvement in change of direction** performance.

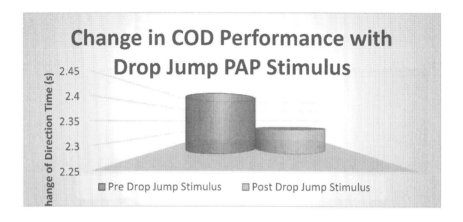

When it comes to subsequent performance augmentation, which is more effective squats, deadlifts, or power cleans?

### Squat vs Deadlift

A 2017 study looking at performance in twenty Rugby players, found that 3 reps at 90+%(of 1RM) in the hex bar deadlift was a suitable, if not more effective alternative, than 3 reps at 90+%(1RM) back squats for **augmenting subsequent countermovement jump performance** (44). Listening to Nike's Senior Director of Performance, Ryan Flaherty, discuss his favorite indicator-lifts, and they use of the hex-bar Deadlift in developing relative strength for NFL and MLB combine athletes –

correlating more specifically to 40 or 60 yard dash times than any other lift.

## Squats vs Power Cleans

Research on college volleyball players set out to determine if squats or power cleans from midthigh were more effective at inducing a positive response in the vertical jump.

The study found the **greatest increase in vertical jump at four minutes after 5 rep set of back squats** and **five minutes after 5 rep set of power cleans,** followed closely by five minutes of rest post back squat (36).

A study on throwers out of the *Carnegie School of Sports in Leeds,* found that strength levels and rest requirements need to be taken into account when using cleans as a means of PAP (17). Likely due to the demand on CNS for a high-load explosive compound lift – using adequate rest should allow for full effort on lighter and faster throws.

**Jump Training for Explosiveness – Tip #4:**

After progressing with the Power-Cut jumps, try doing **a "Speed" jump off and across the front leg** to mimic and improve your explosive cutting ability off that inside leg.

**Also training this type of femoral internal-rotation will help minimize risk of ACL tear by exposing yourself and strengthening a similar the action and injury mechanism.**

**Front Squat vs Back Squat**

Research out of the *Exercise Science Department at East Stroudsburg University* in Pennsylvania looked at the potential differences between front squat and back squat in augmenting forty meter sprint performance.

Subjects participated in four testing sessions, including: a **1RM parallel back squat** baseline session; a **3 rep back squat PAP session**; a **3 rep front squat at 80% back squat PAP session**; and a **control**. After testing, the subjects walked around for 4 minutes, then tested 40m sprints.

Both **squat interventions resulted in greater sprint speeds**, with

> **Jump Training for Explosiveness – Tip #5:**
>
> Adding a simple **"Pop-start" helps to create a reflexive and rapid-fire aspect** to any jump training drills.
>
> **Do this by performing a 1-2" mini jump just before your actual jump drill.** Remembering that stiffness and minimizing the ground contact time is key!

the back squat leading to a slightly better performance than the front squat (58). As we saw in the EMG muscle-activation studies in an earlier chapter, Back vs. Front squat tended to favor linear straight-line speed vs lateral agility speed.

## What about Box Squats?

A 2016 study recruited fourteen elite *French Rugby League Academy* players to determine if paused box squats with bands were an effective method for augmenting standing broad jump performance. After measuring baseline standing broad jump, the experimental group athletes did four sets of 2 paused box squats with bands (a total of 8 reps), resting 90 seconds before performing two standing broad jumps. The control group did the standing broad jumps only (45). *The results are below:*

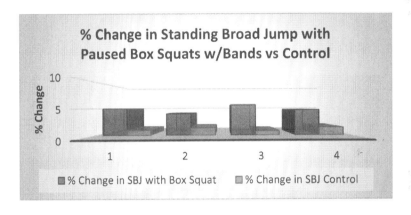

While seeing dramatic performance increases following the squat protocol, one further question remained as we could not help but wonder, **was it the box squat protocol or the accommodating resistance from the bands (or both)?**

To investigate if accommodating resistance squats with bands were more effective than regular back squats, a research team had recreationally trained subjects perform either back squats for three reps at 85%(1RM), accommodating resistance back squats for 3 at 85% (with 30% coming from band resistance), or sit/rest for 5 mins.

9.1 meter sprint performances were evaluated immediately, 1min, 2mins, 3mins and 4 mins after squatting or sitting. **The accommodating resistance squats led to significantly faster sprint times than both control and regular squat at 3 and 4 minutes post** (57).

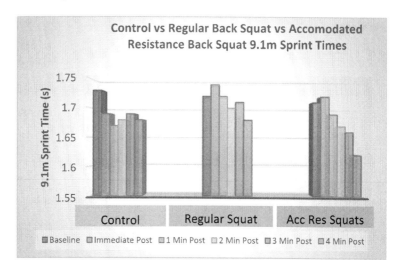

Research from the *International Journal of Sports Physiology and Performance* had similar findings in that broad jump performance was significantly augmented when preceded by accommodating resistance squats (48). Teaching true acceleration through bands / chains versus regular dead weight on the bar is a key to training for sport-specific and explosive strength adaptations.

## What about squat depth? Does it play a role?

A 2013 study on *Rugby Union* players looked at the impacts quarter squatting vs half squatting had on countermovement jump performance. After sets of 3RM quarter and parallel back squats, followed by a five minute rest, the athlete's jumps were tested. The deeper squats led to better outcomes in subsequent jumping performance [20].

## What about clustered sets vs traditional sets?

Researchers looked at the impact a set of 10 clustered reps at 90%(1RM) in the back squat had on 10m and 30m sprint times at different rest durations. Clustered sets are a popular strength protocol based on performing heavy loading, in this case greater than 2-3RM for up 10 reps, more than would usually be physically possible. The technique is made possible by intra-set rests (usually 20-60 seconds) between each repetition, therefore extending the total number of reps beyond what would usually be done.

> **Jump Training for Explosiveness – Tip #6:**
>
> Training the start position from static stretch (paused) at the bottom of the counter-movement helps **create tension in the bigger muscles of the hips and upper-leg prior to an explosive acceleration drill.**
>
> Doing this helps learn any new movement and **teach the body speed in and out of these positions.**

- During the 1st session researchers had 15 athletes from different sports find their best of three 30 meter sprint time to be used as a baseline.

- During the 2nd session: the athletes performed a clustered set of 10 back squats at 90%. They then **rested 3 minutes** and tested their 30m sprint times again.

- During the third and final session the athletes went through the same protocol, but this time **rested 5 minutes** between squats and 30m sprint.

While, the 3 minute rest interval resulted in negligible changes in sprint times, **the 5 minute rest interval sprint times could be the difference between a game winning touchdown and being hit for a loss in the back field (see below)** (9).

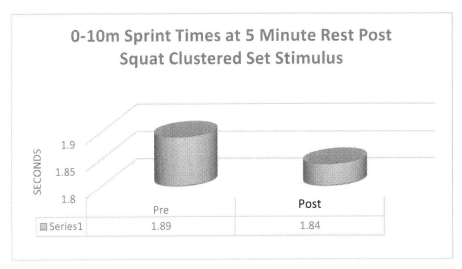

0-10m Sprint Times at 5 Minute Rest Post Squat Clustered Set Stimulus

| | Pre | Post |
|---|---|---|
| Series1 | 1.89 | 1.84 |

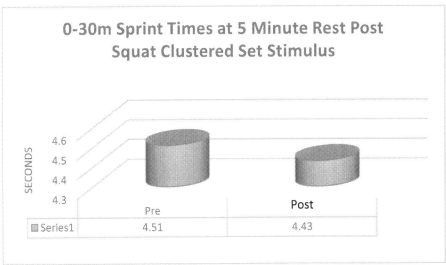

0-30m Sprint Times at 5 Minute Rest Post Squat Clustered Set Stimulus

| | Pre | Post |
|---|---|---|
| Series1 | 4.51 | 4.43 |

In a more recent study from the *Journal of Applied Physiology, Nutrition, and Metabolism,* researchers compared the augmentation of 20m sprints when using **different inter-rep rest periods** for clustered sets.

On three separate occasions, the research team had a group of college soccer players set their baseline 20m sprint time, then perform one of the training protocol's:

- A **straight set** of 3 rep back squat at 85%1RM
- A **clustered set** of 3 at 85% with **30s of rest between each of the reps**
- Or a **clustered set** of 3 at 85% with **60s of rest between each of the reps**.

The athletes were then retested in 20m sprints at 1, 4, 7 and 10 mins post squat set. The **clustered set with 30s rest** led to the best sprint performances 4, 7, and 10 mins post (38). *See below:*

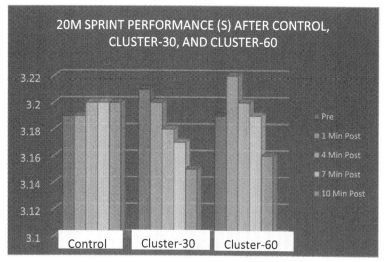

**Can clustered sets augment jumping performance as well?**
In a study on basketball players, athletes performed one of the

following protocols, prior to testing their countermovement vertical jump:

- 3 traditional sets of 6 reps
- or 3 clustered sets of 6 reps with 20 seconds between each of the reps

The countermovement jump was tested at 30s, 4, and 8 mins after the squat set intervention. After both the 4 and 8 minutes of rest, the clustered set of squats led to improved performances in the countermovement jump (28).

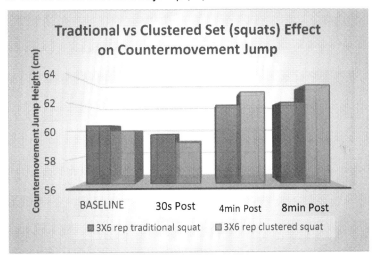

## Eccentric Emphasis/Tempo

A 2019 paper on 24 college football players found that by adding a longer eccentric element (consisting of 5 seconds lowering the bar) to conventional deadlifts, athletes saw greater

77

improvements in their standing broad jumps than when the deadlifts were performed without any tempo at all (7).

## Isometric vs dynamic?

Is one better than the other for stimulus? Researchers out of the *London Sports Institute* found 3 x 3s isometric squats had minimal impact on 5-10-5 performance in Rugby Union players (35). A separate study on college rugby players though, did find a **significant positive correlation between the mid-thigh isometric pull and 1RM back squat, 5 m sprint time, and pro-agility time** (52).

## Resisted Sprinting

A team of researchers looked at the potential PAP benefits resisted sled towing may have in speed and acceleration. After a baseline 30m sprint session, the subjects were required to **sprint thirty meters with 30% of their body mass**. After the sprint they tested non-resisted 30m sprint times after 2, 4, 6, 8, and 12 minutes of rest. Slight improvements were seen at 6, 8, and 12 mins of rest, **peaking at 8 minutes, while a drop in performance was seen at 2 minutes of rest** *(See chart on next page)*

(56). *(If budget allows, two of the best resisted sprint tools on the market are the Run-Rocket and 1080 Sprint.)*

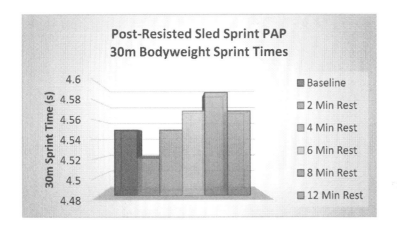

**Jump-Specific Training Machines**: like the *Vertimax (and Supercat)*

*To date there have been 4 studies on Vertimax, with 2 showing positive enhancement results, one showing depth jumps to be more effective, and the final study showed statistically similar results after 6 weeks between Vertimax and non-Vertimax groups.* Here is a quick synopsis of the two positive studies:

The first was a 2008 study out of the *Journal of Strength and Conditioning Research* looked at the addition of resisted jump training in the form of the Vertimax device. Forty Division I collegiate athletes from several different sports participated in a **12 week training program consisting of 2-3 days per week of weight training, and 1-2 days per week of sprints + plyo or sprints + Vertimax training.** The groups tested their baseline

79

countermovement jump power before and after their respective 12 week training cycles (41). The researchers found a **significant difference in power after 12 weeks of training**. Below are the findings:

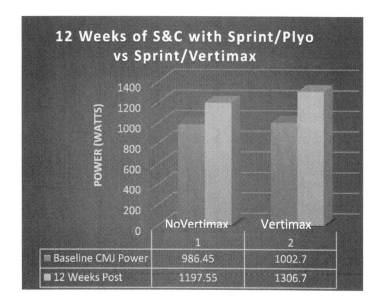

In a similar study, this time with 60 high school athletes from mixed sports, the athletes participated in a **12 week training cycle consisting of 2-3 days per of weights and 1-2 days per week of either sprint/plyo or sprint/Vertimax training**. The results were similar to those in the Division I college athlete study (42). *(See chart on next page).*

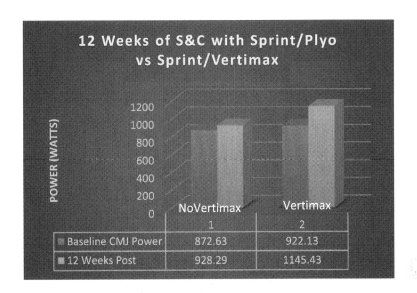

| | NoVertimax 1 | Vertimax 2 |
|---|---|---|
| Baseline CMJ Power | 872.63 | 922.13 |
| 12 Weeks Post | 928.29 | 1145.43 |

**12 Weeks of S&C with Sprint/Plyo vs Sprint/Vertimax**

POWER (WATTS)

From decades of personal coaching experience in using the Vertimax and Supercat with thousands of athletes for nearly two decades, we have seen similar results.

Each machine having its own benefit:

**Hip vs Axial Loading**

- The Vertimax is stretch chord resisted with its patented pulley system underneath to ensure equal resistance throughout the movements. The resistance is placed at the hips, allowing freedom of movement in the upper body.

- The Supercat is plate loaded, with the resistance placed on the shoulders allowing for axial loading of the spine.

**Hip Dominant vs Quad Dominant?**

- Jumps on the Vertimax are done on the flat platform. Athletes can perform a variety of different jumps (quarter jump rebounds, vertical jumps, split jumps, etc). The type of jump chosen allows for greater recruitment of hips vs quads.

- The design of the Supercat allows for squat jumps, but due to the angle of the foot plate, the hip extensors can be more heavily recruited for explosive movement.

---

**Jump Training for Explosiveness – Tip #7:**

Add a med-ball or light weight to your jumping variations. **Any form of weight (including vests) will contribute to overloading the movement in general.**

When in a single-leg or stride stance, the weight will counter-balance to the supporting hip and help **overload at the bottom of the jump and as the arms swing up it will actually assist (via momentum) to complete the top half of the jumping action!**

---

**Measuring Training Progress**

- Methods to track progress on the Supercat:
  - Resistance used
  - Max and Avg jump height per set
  - Watts/Bar Speed (Gymaware, Bar Sensei, etc)
- Methods to track progress on the Vertimax:

82

- Chord setting
- Jump height
- Watts/Bar Speed (Gymaware, Bar Sensei, etc)

When we first started using the Supercat, we had good luck in using the Tendo Powerlyzer unit for tracking and not to forget, instant feedback and some motivational and competitive purposes.

> **Jump Training for Explosiveness – Tip #8:**
>
> Band resisted jumps, anchoring the athlete to a wall or squat rack before **performing broad jumps or linear / lateral bounds helps to provide accommodating resistance to an already explosive exercise.**

For the same experience on the Vertimax, we would incorporate the use of an overhead goal to reach during our sets. A study from 2005 in the *Journal of Strength and Conditioning* Research found overhead goal training led to significant improvements in an athlete vertical jump performance (21). A more recent, 2017, study recommended the use of a virtual target to improve vertical jumping performance (22).

Athletes and coaches have also used the *"goal"* method for horizontal speed training as well, incorporating the ball drop drill into short resisted sprints/accelerations. Suing partners rest intervals to throw and bounce a ball out in front for the trainee to sprint after – timing and regulating speed.

The research seems to point in the direction that resisted, plyometric, and goal training can lead to positive increases in performance.

### Assisted or overspeed work?

To test this, a group of researchers did a study on New Zealand professional *Rugby Union* players. They found **assisted and resisted jumps to be more effective at increasing vertical leap than free jumps after just four weeks of training** (3). A separate study on volleyball players found that assisted jumping utilizing elastic bands improved jump power and height (46).

Throughout the years in knee ankle, knee, hip, and lower back rehab, these assisted jumps are an excellent tool for bringing an athlete back to health and giving them the bounce that they once had pre-injury. This type of assisted stretch-shortening training also de-loads the tissue for conditioning purposes in preparation for

> **Jump Training for Explosiveness – Tip #9:**
>
> Overspeed jumping – using bands rigged overhead and in the athlete's hands or a special vest helps **assist the rapid stretch-shortening cycle (SSC) to enhance the rate of force production**
>
> Increase the ability to pop off the ground allows us to get ahead of competitors from the first step!

heavier-loading or high intensity depth drops and jumps in future training and eventual return to sport.

**Hormonal Impacts**

Both contrast and complex training interventions led to improvements in countermovement jump height, 20m sprint and T-test performance in a 2019 study. The researchers also found **significant increases in Free Testosterone and decreases in Cortisol post-test** *(below)* (30).

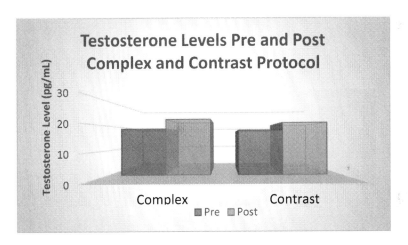

**Can we augment our strength levels in successive sets during the same weight training session?**

Researchers from Brazil set out to investigate if one rep in the back squat at 90%1RM could augment total reps achieved (and power) in 4 successive sets of squats at 70% (with 2 mins rest between sets). Below are the results of the reps achieved in the **first set** at 70% (16).

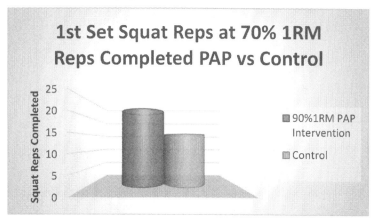

And the total reps for all 4 sets (16).

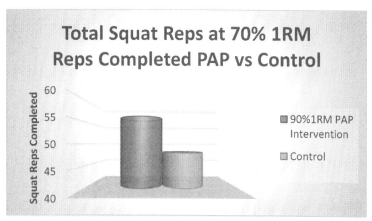

In a similar study, this time testing the upper body, researchers had subjects perform a 90% 1RM bench press, then rest 10 minutes. After the rest, the subjects performed three sets of max reps in the bench press at 70%1RM with 90s of rest between sets (2).

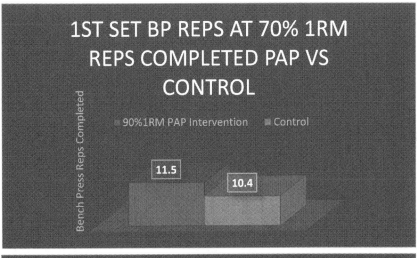

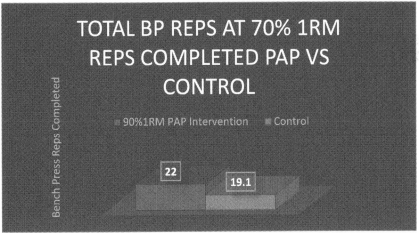

## Specific Sports Applications?

### Golf:

*Can lower and total body potentiation stimulus lead to improvements in rotational movements such as golf swings, lacrosse and hockey shooting, and tennis?* 2013 research out of the UK set out to test this on **golf club head speed**.

During the first session the golfers set their best of three swing speeds as a baseline. They then rested an hour and came back for either the experimental or control test. The experimental group did **3 countermovement jumps**, rested 1 minute, then tested club head speed again. **The three countermovement jumps prior led to nearly a 3mph increase in club head speed** (40).

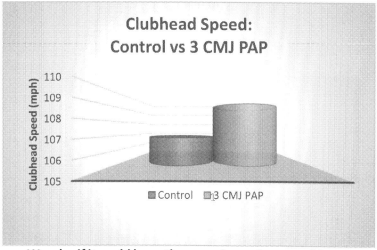

*Wonder if it could have the same impact on punching power and throwing speed?*

## Swimming:

When researchers tested postactivation potentiation training benefits on swimmers, they found moderate improvements in performance for the 100m freestyle after the athletes potentiated with four 10m resisted rack swims (26). It seems the benefits of PAP translate from land to water, making for great immediate performance and training enhancements.

---

**Jump Training for Explosiveness – Tip #11:**

Staying true to the approach of contrast between light and heavy jumping forces, a great combination (due to vertical forces applied) is the circuit of:

**A1-Farmers Carry x 20-40 yards**

**A2-Power Skips x 20   or**

**A2-Verical jump x 3-5 (overhead goal if possible)**

Also for some great PAP the combination of setting the trap bar in front of a plyo box (at height-enough to land above ¼ squat and perform the Box-Jump rep from the bottom of the deadlift:

**A1 – Eccentric Trap/ Hex Bar Deadlift x 1-2 @6seconds**

**A2 – Concentric-only Box Jump x 1 @max height (for ¼ squat) landing)**

---

### Grappling Sports:

Looking at the effects of PAP for grappling sports, a team of researchers had Judo athletes partake in four separate training sessions:

- a plyo-only session,
- a strength session,
- a contrast session, and a
- baseline control group,

The athletes were each evaluated by using a test known as the *Special Judo Fitness Test*. **The *SJFT* consists of the athletes doing as many throws as possible in three separate timed rounds (15, 30, and 30 seconds) with a 10 second rest between rounds**, then testing their heart rate immediately and one minute after. The contrast stimulus led to better performance in both the throws and heart rate testing when preceding the SJFT (37).

A separate study on the *Special Judo Fitness Test*, from 2019 looked further into the PAP effects of **upper body and lower body stimulus vs lower body stimulus vs regular warm up** on the *Special Judo Fitness Test*. **The Upper and lower body stimulus not only led to more power in the high pull test, but it also resulted in nearly one more total rep in the SJFT** (34).

## Soccer:

A 6 week study out of Portugal divided a group of adolescent soccer players into:

- a control group
- a group that utilized complex/contrast training methods once per week
- a third group that utilized contrast/complex methods twice per week.

The researchers tested the athlete's baseline and post 6 week training cycle 15m straight sprint, 15m agility test with the ball, crossing efficacy, and shooting effectiveness. Below are the results of the speed and agility tests in all three groups after 6 weeks of training (1).

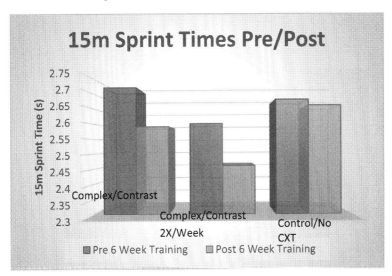

A separate study, this one out of the *Journal of Sports Medicine and Physical Fitness,* found that **8 weeks of bi-weekly contrast training was effective at increasing short sprint and agility performance** in 28 U-17 soccer players (25). That's just 4 total training weeks, showing once again the lasting effects PAP can have on performance with such minimal training dose. Talk about the most bang for your buck training regimen.

### Is there a way or method in which we can organize these to take the greatest advantage of PAP?

French track and field coach Gilles Cometti may have thought so while popularizing the most common contrast method used today by coaches and athletes from all sports.

### *The French Contrast Method*

The *French Contrast Method* is a circuit method that places specific exercise types in a very strategic order to allow for the greatest PAP stimulus results. The exercises are broken down in this way (A1-A4, making a 4-exercise PAP circuit):

> **A1:** Relative Strength/Power Exercise/Heavy Partial/Isometric: Squats, Deadlifts, Power Cleans, Bench Press, etc
>
> **A2:** Force Oriented Plyo (or sprint): Jumps/Plyo, bounding, sprint, resisted sprints, change of direction, etc

**A3**: <u>Dynamic/Speed Strength Exercise:</u> Loaded/resisted jumps, throws, sled pushes, Olympic lift derivatives, speed squats, dynamic bench press, etc

**A4**: <u>Speed or Assisted/Overspeed Exercise:</u> Band assisted jumps, band assisted jump pushups, hurdle hops, etc.

What does the research field say about this method?

A 2018 study out of Spain looked at the immediate potentiation impacts of the *French Contrast Method*. Thirty-one recreational athletes volunteered for the study. After estimating their 1RM squat, the athletes tested their baseline countermovement jumps height.

After baseline was set, 17 subjects rested 2 minutes and started the *French Contrast* potentiation protocol while the control group rested for 15 minutes (27). The protocol is below:

| Experimental French Contrast Protocol: (3 Sets) |
| --- |
| **A1:** 3s Isometric Partial Squat Hold with 85%1RM |
| *Rest 20s* |
| **A2:** Drop Jumps X 3 from 50cm box |
| *Rest 20s* |
| **A3:** Dynamic Half Squats X 3 with 50%1RM |
| *Rest 20s* |
| **A4:** 50cm Hurdle Jumps X 3 (with 1.5m between hurdles) |
| *Rest 5 Mins* |
| **Re-test countermovement jump** |

While the control group saw a decrease in countermovement jump performance, the *French Contrast* group saw significant increases from baseline across all three sets *(results in the following table)*. Bringing more support for the use of techniques such as this for increased PAP benefit.

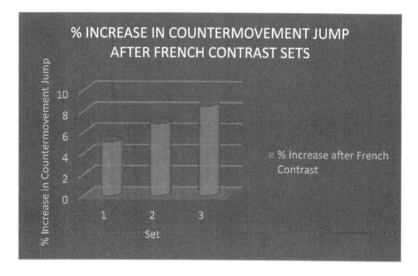

Looking at longer term impacts, a 2019 looked at 8-weeks of training 3X/week using the *French Contrast Method*. The researchers saw a **7.31% increase in the triple jump step and 3.85% increase in triple jump distances** (19). Explosiveness in these tests create an immediate boost to on-field bounce and elusiveness.

A 2019 research study out of *Sacred Heart University* looked at the impacts of 6 weeks of training, twice per week using *French Contrast* training. The researchers saw significant improvements in squat jump and countermovement jump performance (54) using the following protocol:

## SHU Experimental French Contrast Protocol:

| Weeks 1-2 (3 Sets) | Weeks 3-4 (3 Sets) | Weeks 5-6 (3 Sets) |
|---|---|---|
| **A1:** Back Squat 3 x 3 @85% 1RM Rest 10s | **A1:** Back Squat 3 x 2 @87.5% 1RM Rest 10s | **A1:** Back Squat 3 x1 @90% 1RM Rest 10s |
| **A2:** CMJ 3 x 3 Rest 10s | **A2:** CMJ 3 x 4 Rest 10s | **A2:** CMJ 3 x 5 Rest 10s |
| **A3:** Trap Bar Jumps @30% 1RM 3 x 3 Rest 10s | **A3:** Trap Bar Jumps @30% 1RM 3 x 4 Rest 10s | **A3:** Trap Bar Jumps @30% 1RM 3 x 5 Rest 10s |
| **A4:** Band Assisted Jumps 3 x 4 Rest 5 Mins | **A4:** Band Assisted Jumps 3 x 5 Rest 5 Mins | **A4:** Band Assisted Jumps 3 x 6 Rest 5 Mins |

Results of the squat and countermovement jump before and after 6 weeks of training.

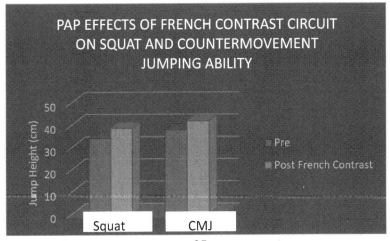

Now that we have looked at the supportive research *(yes there are also studies that show PAP doesn't work)*, what are some program examples?

Squat Example

| Exercise | Reps | Sets | Tempo | Rest Period |
|---|---|---|---|---|
| A1: Back Squat | 2-3 | 5 | 41X1 | 30s |
| A2: Depth Jumps | 3-5 | 5 | X0X0 | 30s |
| A3: Dynamic Squats w/bands | 4-5 | 5 | 10X0 | 30s |
| A4: High Hurdle Hops | 3-5 | 5 | X0X0 | 180s |

Deadlift Example

| Exercise | Reps | Sets | Tempo | Rest Period |
|---|---|---|---|---|
| A1: Hex Bar Deadlift | 2-3 | 5 | 41X1 | 30s |
| A2: Vertical Jump Testing | 2-3 | 5 | X0X0 | 30s |
| A3: Overhead Backward Med Ball or Kettlebell Throw | 3-5 | 5 | X0X0 | 30s |
| A4: Band Assisted Jumps | 3-5 | 5 | X0X0 | 180s |

## Power Clean Example

| Exercise | Reps | Sets | Tempo | Rest Period |
|---|---|---|---|---|
| A1: Power Cleans | 2-3 | 5 | X0X0 | 30s |
| A2: Broad Jump | 2-3 | 5 | X0X0 | 30s |
| A3: Vertimax Quick Jumps | 5 | 5 | X0X0 | 30s |
| A4: Band Assisted Jumps | 3-5 | 5 | X0X0 | 180s |

## Front Squat Example

| Exercise | Reps | Sets | Tempo | Rest |
|---|---|---|---|---|
| A1: Front Squat | 2-3 | 5 | 41X1 | 30s |
| A2: 5-10-5 | 1 | 5 | X0X0 | 30s |
| A3: DB Jump Squats | 3 | 5 | X0X0 | 30s |
| A4: Band Assisted Jumps | 3-5 | 5 | X0X0 | 180s |

## Unilateral Lower Body Example

| Exercise | Reps | Sets | Tempo | Rest |
|---|---|---|---|---|
| A1: Bulgarian Split Squat | 2-3 | 5 | 30X1 | 30s |
| A2: Split Jumps | 2-3/leg | 5 | X0X0 | 30s |
| A3: Alternating Box Step Ups | 2-3/leg | 5 | X0X0 | 30s |
| A4: Overspeed Sprint (10-20m) | 3-5 | 5 | NA | 180s |

## *"Not quite French"* KB Contrast Circuit Example

| Exercise | Reps | Sets | Tempo | Rest |
|---|---|---|---|---|
| A1: KB High Pull from ground | 2-3 | 5 | X0X0 | 30s |
| A2: KB Farmer Carry | 20-50yds | 5 | NA | 30s |
| A3: Overhead Backward Med Ball or KB Throws | 2-5 | 5 | X0X0 | 30s |
| A4: Vertical Jumps with Overhead Goal | 1-3 | 5 | NA | 180s |

# Chapter 4

## *Athlete Recovery*

With all this hard training, athletes need to make sure they are doing everything they can to recover properly. Let's get right to the point here and talk about tools and methods to measure and manage recovery from training.

**Evaluating Recovery**

1. **Morning Grip Strength Test:** In his excellent book, *Science of Sports Training*, sports scientist Thomas Kurz states (29) *"In overstrain, insufficient recovery, and in the initial phase of overtraining, the values of morning dynamometry go down (29)."*

2. **Morning Heart Rate:** Measure your heart rate first thing in the morning before you sit up or get out of bed to determine recovery/readiness to train. The higher your morning heart rate, the harder your body is working to replenish, restore, and detoxify. If your morning heart rate is on the lower end of the scale (<50 bpm), there is a good chance your body is recovered, well rested, and ready to train. For men, over 65 bpm may be a warning sign you need more recovery, while for women over 72 bpm may be a sign to take the day off of training.

3. **Vertical Jump Testing:** A 2017 study out of Cal State Fullerton 17 subjects tested vertical jump height and power then found their 5RM in power cleans and 6RM in push press, back squat, RDL, and leg press.

The next day the subjects came back in, tested vertical, then worked out. They performed 4 sets of 5 reps in the hang clean, 4 sets of 6 repetitions in the push press with 2-minute rest between sets. Both exercises were performed at intensity level to ensure fatigue. Next, subjects did back squat, RDL, and Leg press for 4 sets each to failure. Immediately after the workout vertical jump was tested again.

The third day they came back in, tested vert, hit the same exact workout as the day before, then re-tested vert again.

The researchers found an **8% drop in vertical jump height for over 48 hours post workout**. The vertical jump (VJ) decrement had a significant correlation with a decrease in back squat performance.

According to the researchers *"the ability of VJ height as a sensitive measure of readiness maybe explained by the bimodality of the stretch-shortening cycle (SSC) mechanism.* **Reductions in SSC performance happen immediately during exercise, recovering approximately 2 hours after exercise and demonstrate a secondary reduction 2 days after exercise when muscle damage is the greatest**. *Therefore, the current study demonstrates that* **measuring VJ** *height after a fatiguing workout and before a subsequent workout may be a beneficial tool for monitoring readiness to train (49)."*

4. **Heart Rate Variability (HRV):** (From Lifestyle Hacks and Workouts for Working People)

Your nervous system consists of the Parasympathetic and Sympathetic Nervous Systems. The Sympathetic increases your heart rate while the Parasympathetic slows it down. HRV is the variability between each individual heartbeat, which is under the control of the PNS and SNS. **The healthier, fitter, and more resilient to stress you are, the higher the variability.** The less resilient you are at dealing with stress and pressure, the lower the variability.

This method of monitoring resilience has been used for over 50 years, with some of the original measurements taken in astronauts to see how they dealt with the stresses of space travel. It has since been used by professional and Olympic athletes, military and special forces, SWAT, cardiologists, and more.

The Welltory free app is a good free option for beginners: Welltory Free App, as well as the Oura Ring, and quite possibly the best at home tool is the Omega Wave. Used by the who's who

103

of professional teams and athletes, OmegaWave not only measures your heart rate via chest strap, but it also hooks up to the base of your thumb and your forehead to measure ECG, Omega (DC potential of the brain), neuromuscular, and reaction rate measurements.

This info provides the user with what is called a Window of Trainability and It also tells you your overall readiness to train, your CNS readiness, your cardiac readiness, and your energy supply readiness. This is an excellent tool, though it is not cheap, the unit runs around $213.90, including the first of the required $14.90 monthly subscription. For more on this excellent product check out Omegawave.

## Recovery Methods

If you haven't already picked yourself up a copy of Thomas Kurz's book, Science of Sport Training, you may want to do yourself a favor and go give it a read.

It is from Kurz' book and through internships with the late, great Charles Poliquin, that many of us first learned about grip strength as a recovery measurement tool. Many may have also learned about the

> For more on Charles Poliquin's teachings and some of the best training, nutrition and health information available, check out StrengthSenseiinc.com and The Dojo of Strength.

impact the environment as well as other factors can have on recovery through Charles and/or Kurz' book.

The specifics and details Kurz shares in this book are incredible. For example, he breaks down recovery massage durations by athlete weight, normal vs sauna condition, local vs general duration, sports athlete participates in, techniques used, and more.

Some of the highlights from the recovery section of his book include:

- **Nutrition and Hydration:** (example: *spicy and roasted foods can make an athlete aggressive, while leftovers can make one bloated and passive.*)
- **Sleep and sleeping environment**
- **The environment:**
  - Swimming in lake, river, or ocean water improves functioning of the nervous system (also helps with arthritis pain and thermo-regulation)
  - Exposure to ocean air with high iodine content improves breathing
  - Sunshine helps circulation, blood pressure, and stimulates the nervous system and metabolism
  - Cloudy day air may improve lung ventilation and regulates nervous system.

- **Listening to relaxing, calming music** for up to 30 minutes post workout
- **Colors**

in your training environment and the physiological and psychological impacts different colors. There have been instances of high-level European soccer players performing particularly bad against teams in yellow – cueing the use of specialized eye-wear / training glasses tinted yellow to help eliminate any inhibitory psychological response.

Some combine prep coaches do the opposite. They utilize glasses of different color to test and find which color is excitatory to an athlete by testing vertical jump height with each color. When the indicator color is found they utilize those glasses on top of their contrast, potentiation and/or cluster training to adapt and create the ultimate training environment.

- **Massage:**

Broken down into Workout massage, Preventive massage, Recovery/regenerative massage, Therapeutic massage, and Sports massage

- **Showers, warm and hot baths, whirlpool, steam bath, and sauna.**
- **Incorporating recovery into macrocycle**:

Kurz recommends during general prep period, cool or lukewarm showers in the morning; warm-cool showers after strength workouts; cool-warm-cool showers after sprint/endurance workouts; and massage and/or warm bath 2-3 times per week after a workout.

During the special prep period, Kurz recommends more local measures including massage, compresses, and heating; if athletes do not sweat during workouts, hot baths or sauna 2-3 times per week.

## Other recovery methods include:

## o  Grounding / Earthing:

*"Environmental medicine focuses on interactions between human health and the environment, including factors such as compromised air and water and toxic chemicals, and how they cause or mediate disease. Omnipresent throughout the environment is a surprisingly beneficial, yet overlooked **global resource for health maintenance, disease prevention, and clinical therapy: the surface of the Earth itself** (48).*

**Check out a wide variety grounding / earthing products at www.ultimatelongevity.com**

Using the electrical ground plug in your home outlets!

There are a variety of products, from pillowcases, sheets, throw blankets and mats.

*Mounting evidence suggests that the **Earth's negative potential can create a stable internal bioelectrical environment*** *for the normal functioning of all body systems. Moreover, oscillations of the intensity of the Earth's potential may be important for setting the biological clocks regulating diurnal body rhythms, such as cortisol secretion* (39)

## o **Vibrational Foam rolling**

Several studies have shown that vibrational foam rolling at a specific megahertz may improve microcirculation and decrease DOMS (delayed onset muscle soreness). – side note: vibrational foam rolling is a great tool for stimulating the reflexology points on the bottom of the feet and can also be great for alleviating Achilles tendon soreness. Check out Hyperice for one of the top product brands on the market.

## o **Cold or contrast water exposure**

A 2010 paper discussed how water immersion can aid in nutrient distribution, reducing muscle edema, getting rid of waste products, increasing cardiac output, and more.

The author expressed *"Water immersion appears to affect a similar physiological response to active recovery without the need to expend extra energy. When a body or a large portion of it is immersed, hydrostatic pressure acts on the body's fluid within the immersed region. Fluid from the extravascular space now moves into the vascular compartment, reducing exercise-induced increase in muscle volume and also reducing soft tissue*

108

*inflammation. The blood volume increase is redistributed to increase the cardiac preload, stroke volume, cardiac output, and blood flow through the body. The cardiac output increases in relation to the depth of immersion and has been observed to increase by as much as 102% during head-out immersions. These cardiovascular responses occur without any increase in energy expenditure (30)."*

Using contrast temperatures led to a greater reduction in blood lactate levels, while ending with cold can encourage vasoconstriction (30). *(I also hear it makes hair shinier).*

> Curcumin, a phytonutrient found in turmeric, is known for its high antioxidant capacity. Studies have shown it may be effective in decreasing oxidative stress, inflammation, muscle damage, and soreness (1,7).
>
> Two forms that have been shown to be effective are *Meriva* (Cuomo 2011), found in Thorne's Meriva sustained release, and Aurea Biolabs Cureit (1).

## ○ Concentric only active recovery training

Popularized by strength coach extraordinaire Louie Simmons of Westside Barbell, concentric only training consists of sled work, prowler work, and non-motorized treadmill work. Swimming and biking are also forms of concentric only exercise.

To induce significant muscle soreness, a 2006 study had subjects perform 60 maximal eccentric only curls on both arms. To test the benefits of concentric only active recovery, the subjects then performed light concentric only curls and extensions on one arm only over the following 4 days.

The researchers found roughly 40% decreases in muscle tenderness and soreness. There was a slight increase in range of motion, however, there was also a slight decrease in strength (51).

> Vitamin C may play a role in recovery from workouts. According to a recent meta-analysis on vitamin C supplementation, it has been found to have a positive impact on the inflammation induced from a single session of exercise (41).

An added benefit of concentric only training is that it may increase lean mass and muscle thickness. A study out of the *European Journal of Applied Physiology* had untrained subjects perform concentric only DB shoulder presses and curls to failure (8-12 reps) twice a week for four weeks on one arm only. The other arm was the control arm.

During the fourth week, subjects showed increases in lean muscle mass and small, but positive improvements in muscle thickness in the trained arm while the control arm showed no improvements (44).

## o Water/Pool "Active Recovery Training"?

A best of both world method? Low impact, concentric dominant, and water immersion combined!

Years ago, one of the greatest Olympic Weightlifters of all-time, Alexeyev, discussed his training method of working with a barbell in the water. *(A picture has also circulated the internet, with Alexeyev cleaning a bar out of the water in a river in Russia).*

The great sport scientist and author of *SuperTraining*, Mel Siff, had the opportunity to discuss various training methodologies with Alexeyev.

**From a 2017 interview article** with Mel Siff on EliteFTS.com titled *The Science of Winning According to Vasili Alexeyev*, Alexeyev expressed to Siff *"When I joined the weightlifting section, there were no sharp definitions between the methods of training. I was not used to training mechanically and I didn't like this. I began to think for myself, how to organize an effective system of training. I knew from my own experience that, with stubborn effort, one can do anything. I didn't spare myself. I worked with maximum weights, analyzed my situation, and again began training. I invented many things myself. For example, I began to work a great deal with the barbell in water.*

*I searched and experimented and here is the result. I made my way from 500 to 600 kilograms in three years. From then on I wanted to be first (25)."*

Siff expressed that bands, chains, and yes, lifting against the variable resistance of water *"can be a useful supplementary form of training* (25)".

Most trainees are not about to bring a barbell and weights to the pool, ocean, or lake. A viable substitute might be a Slamball medicine ball.

Overhead medicine ball throws out of waist to sternum height water. Squat jump chest pass medicine balls from similar depth. Over the shoulder tosses. Lateral slamdowns. Split jump and single leg chest pass throws. If you have a pool you can do these in the privacy of your own back yard without ruining a barbell or plates.

From our experiences, many athletes enjoy the unorthodox approach, and have told us over the years that they love this form of training and feel more explosive and less beat up from the weeks of a rigorous training cycle.

## o Massage

A systematic review and meta-analysis on recovery methods found massage to be the best tool for reducing inflammation, decreasing DOMS, and recovering from fatigue. Cold immersion and

Caffeine has been shown to have a positive impact on DOMS. Interestingly it may have a greater effect on males than females. A 2019 study from the *Journal of Applied Physiology* had elite male and female college athletes take either 6mg/kg of caffeine or a placebo for 24 and 48 hours after a DOMS inducing workout. The researchers found that the group taking caffeine had lower levels of delayed muscle soreness and better performance in max voluntary contraction testing, with the male athletes showing significantly better improvements (8). A separate study from the *Journal of Pain* had similar findings (34).

compression garments were also effective methods for decreasing inflammation, soreness, and fatigue. Cryotherapy, contrast water therapy, and active recovery were also effective tools in decreasing DOMS (13).

## o **Sleep**

How important is sleep?

*Hormones:* affected by sleep: Growth hormone, Insulin, Thyroid, Satiety Hormones, Testosterone and Testosterone precursors etc

*Brain:* the glymphatic system is your brains "drainage" system, clearing metabolites that have accumulated throughout the day. This process occurs when you sleep.

*Detoxification:* Phase I and Phase II of detoxification occur at night while sleeping.

*Muscle:* recovery and rebuilding occur while sleeping via enhanced muscle protein synthesis

*Injury Prevention:* Sleeping less than 8 hours per night increases injury risk in adolescent athletes by 1.7x (almost twice as much!) (37)

*Nervous system:* recovery occurs during deep sleep phases.

***Immune System:*** recovery occurs overnight following the healing effects from the cascade of other benefits listed.

## o **Sensory deprivation bath**

Alone with just your own thoughts in your head. That is the first thing noticed when we were introduced to these back in 2001. Lying in this giant bathtub, filled with 98.5 degree water and Dead Sea Salt, earplugs in, complete darkness, and not a scent to be found.

A 2014 study had subjects participate in 7 weeks of sensory isolation flotation. Via questionnaire, the researcher found significant **improvements in sleep, stress, anxiety, and pain** (28).

A separate study looked at the impacts on muscle pain only. After three weeks of sensory isolation flotation, the subjects saw a **significant decrease in severe head and neck pain.** Another benefit the researchers found: the sensory isolation flotation **subjects also slept much better** (27).

## o **Yoga**

Yoga has been shown to improve symptoms of chronic pain and stress, enhance cardiovascular function, strength, and flexibility, and improve general overall well-being (50). Hot yoga has the added benefit of increased perspiration and associated detoxification.

### o **Ozone Sauna/Therapy**

Ozone therapy has been shown to increase ATP and may increase cellular metabolism due to its positive impacts on the mitochondria. It has also been shown to improve blood circulation and oxygen delivery to ischemic tissues as well as improve immune function.

According to a 2017 study, *"A plethora of laboratory studies have provided evidence of O3's antioxidant capabilities, as well as vascular, hematological, and immune system modulations. This evidence has been further substantiated in clinical trials with O3 therapy being* **useful in the cardiovascular, subcutaneous tissue, peripheral vascular disease, neurological, head and neck, orthopedic, gastrointestinal, and genitourinary pathologies.** *O3 therapy has proven especially* **beneficial in the diabetic foot, ischemic wounds, and peripheral vascular disease,** *areas in which O3 use is most prevalent (43)."*

Check out the best-selling Ozone Sauna by Longevity Resources here.

## o **Hyperbaric Chamber Therapy**

Hyperbaric chambers fully enclosed capsules that administer 100% oxygen at a high atmospheric pressure. They have been used for years with the intention of increasing the oxygen carrying capacity of red blood cells.

More recently they have been used for soft tissue and injury recovery due to their potential impacts on inflammation and swelling.

A 2016 looked at the impact two hours of hyperbaric oxygen therapy had on recovery in Brazilian jiu-jitsu athletes. The **athletes who used the hyperbaric chamber had slightly lower lactate levels and significantly better rating of perceived recovery** (RPR) (6).

While venomous spiders are the last topic we thought to bring into this book – it found a way to fit in! Specifically, pertaining to the treatment of poisonous spider bites. It appears that the science world may have also found some credibility to the hyperbaric chamber treatment for these bites, with studies dating back as far as 1991.

A 2016 study had subjects who had undergone 2-3 months of antibiotics, dressings, and corticosteroids yet still had non-healing wounds from brown spider bites, go through daily hyperbaric oxygen therapy treatments.

After 13 sessions, the wound completely healed in the youngest subject (30yrs old) while it took 30 sessions for complete healing in the 70 year old subject. None of the subjects required surgery or further treatments (21).

If you are interested in setting one up, Oxygen Health Systems offers both rental and purchasing options.

## o  **Cryotherapy:**

A 2017 review of the scientific literature on whole body cryotherapy pointed out positive results including:

- o Improvements in perception of pain and tiredness after 1, 24, and 48hrs hours post workout session (33).
- o **40% decrease in the inflammatory biomarker** creatine kinase after just 5 cryotherapy sessions (33).
- o Improvement **sleep quality**, which led to an increased tolerance of greater training loads (33).
- o **Increases in testosterone levels** when cryotherapy was used as a recovery after 20 minutes of intense sprints. This increased testosterone led improvements in testosterone to cortisol ratios (33).

The authors expressed *"in addition to beneficial effects on inflammation and muscle damage, WBC induces peripheral vasoconstriction, which **improves muscle oxygenation, lowers***

117

*submaximal heart rate and increases stroke volume, stimulates autonomic nervous parasympathetic activity and increases norepinephrine* (33)."

○ **Photobiomodulation** (*red light therapy*)

Also known as low-level laser therapy (LLLT) or light-emitting diode therapy (LEDT). A few decades ago, NASA found that specific wavelengths of red light could potentially have positive health benefits. From then on, researchers have been studying this form of recovery therapy. They have found:

> Photobiomudulation may **increase muscle fiber excitability and aid in muscle repair and recovery** (16).

Red or near-infrared Photobiomodulation can **improve energy levels** through its stimulatory effects on mitochondrial activity and may increase ATP levels (16).

Red-light therapy has also been shown to increase testosterone and may be useful as treatment for male infertility. 2016 research on low sexual desire subjects use a light box first thing in the morning found a **71% increase in testosterone levels after just 2 weeks** of light box therapy (14).

Photobiomudulation may **decrease oxidative stress levels** (16).

Check out Joovv for a full line of red light therapy products from the Joovv Mini all the way up to the Joovv Elite.

## o  Probiotics/Gut Health:

A 2016 study found that taking the probiotic Bacillus coagulans GB-30,6086 with protein increased levels of perceived recovery and decreased levels of perceived soreness 24, 48, and 72 hours post strenuous leg workout (26).

The same study found a marked difference in the muscle inflammation biomarker creatine kinase (CK), with the protein only group seeing a 261% increase in CK, while the group taking the probiotics with the protein saw that number cut nearly in half, at a 137% increase.

A third finding of the study was the results of the 30s Wingate power test. The group taking the protein only saw 5.3% drop in power, while the probiotic + protein group actually saw an increase in power.

Blueberries, specifically those from New Zealand, have shown in research decrease oxidative stress levels and improve recovery rates after a strenuous eccentric based workout (36).

The researchers believed these positive results were due to the fact that *"Bacillus coagulans GBI-30, 6086 enhances the health of the cells of the gut lining improving nutrient absorption including minerals, peptides and amino acids by decreasing inflammation and encouraging optimum development of the absorptive area of the villi (26)."*

Research has also shown that probiotics can be an effective tool in fending off gastrointestinal issues and upper respiratory infections in high level athletes (18,23,42).

119

So profound are the potential positive impacts of certain probiotic strains *(Bacillus coagulans GBI-30,6086)* that a 2014 study actually found a significantly greater increase in vertical jump power (after 8 weeks of training) in the group ingesting probiotic + protein as compared with the group taking protein only (17).

For much more on probiotics including in depth discussion on positive benefits, specific strains to look for, what brands contain what strains, and best times to take them check out the book Lifestyle Hacks and Workouts for Working People.

- ## Fish Oil

Fish oil has long been touted for its beneficial effects on cardiovascular health and inflammation. A 2017 randomized, placebo-controlled, double-blind study found that taking 6 grams/day of fish oil for one week prior to a 10 sets, to failure, workout led to significantly lower levels of perceived functional and static muscle soreness (45). Other studies have had similar findings (11,52).

A 2007 meta-analysis found that supplementing with fish oil for 3-4 months decreased joint pain and morning stiffness (19), while a recent 10 week study on endurance athletes found significantly lower inflammatory biomarker numbers in athletes taking concentrated DHA and EPA versus those taking a placebo (40).

Fish oil can also help with immune recovery post workout. A study out of *Brain Behavior and Immunity* looked at the impact 3 grams per day of fish oil had on post workout immune response after an hour long cycling workout. The group taking the fish oil had more had a much greater increase in immune response biomarkers than the group taking the placebo (20).

A few high quality fish oil products to check out include:

- Poliquin EPA-DHA 720 TG: This one has 2,722mg of ultra-pure fish oil including 860mg EPA and 580mg DHA
- Thorne Research Super EPA Pro: contains 320mg DHA and 1300mg EPA. Thorne also makes great heart health product with their Omega-3 w/ CoQ10.

o **Panax Ginseng**

Want to increase muscle activation and decrease perceived effort? Panax Ginseng may help.

A 2020 double blind, crossover study on track athletes found that taking Panax Ginseng four days prior to a grueling squat workout could decrease the rate of perceived exertion while increasing EMG activity of the working muscles.

The subjects continued to supplement with the Ginseng for another three days (8 days total) while testing maximal isometric contraction (MVIC), EMG, lactate, and muscle damage biomarkers. **The athletes taking the Panax Ginseng not only saw greater EMG activity in their working muscles, but they also saw significantly higher isometric contraction forces 24, 48, and 72 hours post workout** (9).

Ron Teegarden's Dragonherbs.com is one of the best Chinese medicine websites for ginseng and many other herbals. They have everything from several different types of Ginseng to super potency Deer Antler Drops to Polyrachis Ant to Reishi mushroom, Tongkat Ali and more.

- ○ **HMB**

What is HMB? β-hydroxy-β-methylbutyrate? HMB is a chemical produced when the amino acid leucine is broken down in the body.  In a recent double blind, placebo controlled study, researchers recruited 20 *"unlucky"* subjects to participate in a six sets of 10, max effort eccentric dumbbell curl DOMS inducing workout. Half the group took 1.5g of HMB for two weeks prior to the workout while the other half took a placebo.

The researchers looked at muscle soreness, stiffness, arm circumference, max voluntary contraction, and range of motion before and immediately after the workout as well as the following five days.

**The group that took the HMB had significantly greater ranges of motion and higher voluntary contraction force immediately, three, and five days after the workout** (46).

Taking 1gm of HMB prior to and after strength workouts as well as 1gm after dinner may aid in muscle recovery and prevent breakdown. Recent research has pointed out the differences between the **calcium version and the free acid version, with the free acid version** potentially carrying a higher potency.

A 2010 double-blind, placebo controlled study found a key antioxidant found in black tea, theaflavin, when taken before exercise, decreased delayed muscle soreness and increased recovery from the Wingate test and 10s sprint intervals (3).

Muscletech's Clear Muscle is one product that contains the free-acid version of HMB.

## ○ BCAA's

Leucine, Isoleucine, and Valine. These three amino acids have been known for their role in muscle building and protein synthesis. They have also been known for their role in hormone and energy production as well as potential impacts on the brain.

A 2019 meta-analysis looked at the impact BCAA ingestion during and following workouts had on delayed onset muscle soreness. The researchers found a significant decrease in DOMS in subjects taking BCAA's with largest the magnitude of the effect appearing 48 hours after exercise (15).

## ○ Riboflavin *(B2)*

A double-blind, placebo-controlled study on ultramarathoners (161.3km race) had a group of runners take 100mg of riboflavin (B2) or placebo a half hour-hour before the race, and again 11-16 hours later, halfway through the race (race took about 20-30hrs). After finishing the race, the participants had their muscle damage and pain levels evaluated.

In the days following the race, the runners who took the riboflavin had lower levels of muscle pain and soreness, as well as better improvements in functional capacity. The researchers theorized the antioxidant properties of riboflavin and/or the *"mitochondrial protective function of riboflavin"* could have played a role in the increased recovery and decreased pain and soreness (24).

Another positive benefit to come out of the study was that those participants that completed the pre-race data collection were given a free t-shirt, and those that completed the entire study, including finishing the 161.3km race, were given a $50 gift certificate.

## ○ Cherries *(Tart)*

Aside from their benefits on cardiovascular health, gout, and rheumatoid arthritis, **Montmorency tart cherries** have been shown to accelerate recovery rates from intense, exercise induced muscle damaging workouts. Researchers theorize *"the cause of this attenuation appears to be related to the antioxidant compound anthocyanin, which is abundant in dark-colored fruits and plants and, especially, cherries and, also, to other phenolic compounds, such as quercetin (31)."*

Tahiti Trader Tart Cherry Organic is a quality, drinkable option.

Blackcurrants, which are also rich in anthocyanins may have similar effects. Studies have found lower levels of the muscle damage biomarker Creatine Kinase in subjects taking blackcurrant juice prior to intense muscle damaging workouts (10,31). R.W. Knudsen makes a blackcurrant juice you can buy at most local grocery stores.

Pomegranate, with its high levels of antioxidants may also play a role in minimizing soreness and muscle damage (2).

## o **Proteolytic Enzymes**

Proteolytic enzymes are naturally occurring enzymes found in the body as well as certain plants, fruits, and even insects. Papain (found in papaya), bromelain (found in pineapple), trypsin, pancreatin, and chymotrypsin are the most common. Cacoonase is a proteolytic enzyme found in the naturally in the silkworm while Wobenzym is made from the combination of trypsin, bromelain and rutoside trihydrate (from the Japanese pagoda tree).

A research team looked at the impact Mango Leaf extract *(and Quercetin)* had on exercise induced muscle damage. To induce muscle damage and soreness, the researchers had endurance trained subjects **run a 10k race, then perform 100 drop jumps**. (Knees are sore just thinking about this.)

For one hour prior to and every 8 hours post workout (for 24 hours), half the subjects took the mango leaf extract and quercetin while the other half took a placebo. The group taking the mango and quercetin had lower levels of muscle pain and muscle damage versus those taking the placebo (35).

A study from the Journal of Sports Sciences found that roughly 4 grams of a mixed protease supplement consisting of trypsin, papain, bromelain, amylase, chymotrypsin, lipase, and lysozyme led to decreased soreness and quicker functional recovery in subjects who ran downhill for 30 minutes at 80% of their maximal heart rate (37).

One of the best products we have come across that contained proteases (but no longer manufactured) was Poliquin's Joint Task Force. We haven't found a product that matches the ingredients and pain management since they stopped making it.

- o **Pre-cooling**

Cooling your body down or decreasing your body temperature before training in the heat. For years we have seen athletes hop in cold pools or take cold showers to get their body temps down prior to summer sprint, prowler, or physical conditioning workouts. Some athletes have used this before karate or wrestling practice to their advantage on hot days.

The theory is this creates a larger heat storage capacity. In research, many pre-cooling techniques have been shown to be effective, with cold water immersion and ice slurry ingestion being two of the best singular modalities, followed by cold air exposure, cooling vests, cooling packs, and drinking cold water (4,5).

According to a 2017 study, *"mixed method cooling appeared to be the most effective strategy to enhance exercise performance, followed by cold water immersion, cold water/ice slurry ingestion, cooling packs and cooling vests. These findings suggest that vigorous cooling of a large surface of the body is more effective than local body and/or less powerful cooling techniques to improve exercise performance* (5)."

A meta-analysis on pre and per-cooling (cooling during exercise) found that pre-cooling significantly improved interval sprint performance. The per-cooling led to nearly a 10% improvement in performance (6).

# Chapter 5

## Organizing a Training Schedule

## Putting it all together:

Training splits can vary widely, from the classic "bro-split" (excluding leg-day is never recommended), to the hard-core train every single day protocols (likely not sustainable for the long term), he versatile 3-day total body split is a favorite (3 days in the weight room – usually 2-3 strongman or speed / agility / conditioning days), or the option of a 4-day upper / lower split, and this list can go on forever.

The most important piece of the equation is training with a direction to begin with. Most high school and college athletes think of a program as too regimented or even just simply want results too fast, including those guys simply *"chasing the pump"* day to day, or the young ladies trying to *"tone up"*.

Whether you are trying to make the team, move up from JV, move on to college, return from an injury, or simply gain a competitive edge on the field – training smarter, not harder is going to be important. The routine that encompasses a bit of everything for an athlete that has less experience is a safe choice, the constant development of General Physical Preparedness (GPP) is a huge factor in both strength and conditioning development long term.

As we talked about earlier in several chapters the development of speed and specifically explosiveness is key to not only making it onto the field, but also making an impact once you are on there. We need general function and movement qualities, on top of the ability to perform these tasks tirelessly. Once easy fundamental human movements are engrained and become "muscle memory", it is safe to say you have generally prepared yourself physically (via GPP) to begin specifying on sports techniques and specific fundamentals to play and perform in that way.

If you cannot do 2-a-day training here is a basic off-season schedule/program example *(taking advantage of PAP)* to get you or your team started.

### Monday: Olympic Lift/Lower Body

| Exercise | Reps | Sets | Tempo | Rest |
|---|---|---|---|---|
| A1: Power Clean from hang above knee | 3-5 | 5 | X0X0 | 45-60s |
| A2: Broad Jump | 2-3 | 5 | NA | 90s |
| B1: Paused Back Squat w/chains | 4-6 | 4 | 31X1 | 45-60s |
| B2: Barbell Jump Squats w/dorsiflexion in air | 2-4 | 4 | NA | 90s |
| C1: Glute Ham Raise | 4-6 | 4 | 4010 | 60s |
| C2: Alternating Leg Step Forward Lunges | 12-16 (total) | 4 | 2010 | 60s |

### Tuesday: Acceleration or Hill Sprints

| Sprint Type | Reps | Rest Period |
|---|---|---|
| 15yd Sprint (use farmers carry for PAP augmentation) | 6-10 (autoregulated at 5% best time drop off) | 60s |
| 30yd Sprint | 4-10 (autoregulated at 5% best time drop off) | 90s |
| Hill Sprint (20-40yds) | 2-6 (autoregulated at 5-10% best time drop off) | 90-120s |

## Wednesday: Upper Body

| Exercise | Reps | Sets | Tempo | Rest |
|---|---|---|---|---|
| A1: Push Press | 3-5 | 5 | 21X1 | 120s |
| B1: Flat Fat Grip Barbell Bench Press w/chains | 3-5 | 4 | 31X1 | 45-60s |
| B2: Kneeling Chest Pass Med Ball Throw | 3 | 4 | NA | 60s |
| B3: Weighted Chin Ups | 3-5 | 4 | 3111 | 45-60s |
| B4: Rotational Med Ball Slamdowns (w/slamball) | 4-6 | 4 | NA | 90s |
| C1: V Bar Dips | 6-8 | 3 | 3112 | 60s |
| C2: Seated Cable Rows | 6-8 | 3 | 4011 | 60s |
| C3: Fat Grip Farmer Carry | 20-40ft | 3 | NA | 90s |

## Thursday: Max Speed

| Sprint Type | Reps | Rest Period |
|---|---|---|
| 40yd Sprint | 4-8 (autoregulated at 5% best time drop off) | 120s |
| 60yd Sprint | 2-6 (autoregulated at 5-10% best time drop off) | 120s |
| 80yd Sprint | 1-2 | 120s |

## Friday: Total Body Weights

| Exercise | Reps | Sets | Tempo | Rest |
|---|---|---|---|---|
| A1: Hex Bar Deadlift | 3-5 | 5 | 31X1 | 45-60s |
| A2: Overhead Med Ball or Kettlebell Throws | 2-4 | 5 | NA | 60s |
| B1: Incline Semi-Pronated Grip DB Bench Press | 4-6 | 4 | 3010 | 45-60s |
| B2: Jump Pushups | 2-5 | 4 | 42X1 | 60s |
| B3: Pull-Ups | 4-6 | 4 | 3010 | 45-60s |
| B4: Slamdowns | 4-5 | 4 | NA | 90s |
| C1: Seated DB External Rotator | 8-10 | 3 | 4010 | 45s |
| C2: Single Arm DB Trap-3 Lift | 8-10 | 3 | 4010 | 45s |

## Saturday: Sled Pushing or Resisted Sprinting

## Sled Push Option

| Sprint Type | Reps | Rest Period |
|---|---|---|
| 10yd Sled Push @ 40-60%BM | 6-10 | 90-120s |
| 20yd Sled Push @10-40%BM | 2-8 | 90-120s |

**Resisted Sprint Option**

| Sprint Type | Reps | Rest Period |
|---|---|---|
| 15yd Resisted Sprint @ 60-70%BM | 6-10 | 90-120s |
| 30yd Resisted Sprint @20-40%BM | 2-8 | 90-120s |

## Sunday: Off

If you prefer to do all your plyo and jump training in the beginning of your leg workout prior to hitting the weights here is an example:

**Monday: Olympic Lift/Lower Body**

| Exercise | Reps | Sets | Tempo | Rest |
|---|---|---|---|---|
| A: Resisted Broad Jump (after last set rest 30s and perform 3-4 consecutive non-resisted broad jumps) | 1 | 5 | NA | 60s |
| B: Single Leg Resisted Broad Jump | 1/leg | 4 | NA | 30s |
| C: Resisted Power Skips (after last set rest 30s and perform 4-6 non-resisted power skips) | 4-6 | 4 | NA | 60s |
| D1: Power Clean from Hang above knee | 3-5 | 5 | X0X0 | 120s |
| E1: Paused Back Squat w/chains | 4-6 | 4 | 31X1 | 45-60s |
| F1: Glute Ham Raise | 4-6 | 4 | 4010 | 60s |
| F2: Alternating Leg Step Forward Lunges | 12-16 (total) | 4 | 2010 | 60s |

# Explosive Athlete

# Sample One-Year Football S&C Program

| Dec | Jan | Feb | Mar | Apr | May |
|------|------|------|------|------|------|
| Phase 1 | Phase 2 | Phase 3 | Phase 4 | Phase 5 | Phase 6 |
| Structural Balance | Accum | Intensification | DUP 1: Strength Density 20 Rep | DUP 2: Waveload Strongman Hypertrophy | DUP 3: Str. Density Strongman Supersets |
| Cond: General Activity | Cond: Genera Activit | Cond: **200m Ev:** Sk:30s, L:35s **120yd Shuttle** Sk:28s L: 33s | Cond: **200m Ev:** Sk:29s, L:33s **120yd Shuttle** Sk:27s L: 33s | Cond: **200m Ev:** Sk:27s, L:32s **120yd Shuttle** Sk:26s L: 33s | Cond: **200m Ev:** Sk:26s, L:31s **120yd Shuttle** Sk:25s L: 32s |

| June | July | Aug | Sept | Oct | Nov |
|------|------|------|------|------|------|
| Phase 7 | Phase 8 | Phase 9 | Phase 10 | Phase 11 | Phase 12 |
| Pre-Summer: Structural Balance | Summer 1 2-a-day | Summer 2 2-a-day | In-Season 1 | In-Season 2 | In-Season 3 |
| Cond: Summer Prep | Cond: Summer SAC Phase 1 | Cond: Summer SAC Phase 2 | Cond: Practice | Cond: Practice | Cond: Practice |

# *EA* Sample One-Year Football S&C Program: **PHASE 1**

# STRUCTURAL BALANCE

## Duration: 4 Weeks
## Frequency: 3x/week

## Optimal Schedule:

| Monday | Tuesday | Wednesday | Thursday | Friday | Saturday | Sunday |
|--------|---------|-----------|----------|--------|----------|--------|
| Structural Balance Day 1 | Off/recovery methods | Structural Balance Day 2 | Off/recovery methods | Structural Balance Day 3 | Off/recovery methods | Off/recovery methods |

# _EA_ Football Phase 1: Day 1: Structural Balance

| Week | Reps | Sets | Tempo | Rest |
|------|------|------|-------|------|
| **A1: FFE Dumbbell Split Squats** | | | | |
| Wk 1 | 10-12/leg | 3 | 4010 | 60s |
| Wk 2 | 9-11/leg | 3 | 4010 | 50s |
| Wk 3 | 8-10/leg | 3 | 4010 | 45s |
| Wk 4 | 7-9/leg | 2 | 4010 | 40s |
| **A2: Chin Ups** | | | | |
| Wk 1 | 10-12 | 3 | 3010 | 60s |
| Wk 2 | 9-11 | 3 | 3010 | 50s |
| Wk 3 | 8-10 | 3 | 3010 | 45s |
| Wk 4 | 7-9 | 2 | 3010 | 40s |
| **B1: Swiss Ball Hamstring Curls** | | | | |
| Wk 1 | 7-9 | 3 | 4010 | 60s |
| Wk 2 | 8-10 | 3 | 4010 | 50s |
| Wk 3 | 9-11 | 3 | 4010 | 45s |
| Wk 4 | 10-12 | 2 | 4010 | 40s |
| **B2: Incline Dumbbell Bench Press** | | | | |
| Wk 1 | 10-12 | 3 | 4010 | 60s |
| Wk 2 | 9-11 | 3 | 4010 | 50s |
| Wk 3 | 8-10 | 3 | 4010 | 45s |
| Wk 4 | 7-9 | 2 | 4010 | 40s |
| **C1: Upright Rows** | | | | |
| Wk 1 | 10-12 | 3 | 2010 | 60s |
| Wk 2 | 9-11 | 3 | 2010 | 50s |
| Wk 3 | 8-10 | 3 | 2010 | 45s |
| Wk 4 | 7-9 | 2 | 2010 | 40s |
| **C2: Low Back Extensions** | | | | |
| Wk 1 | 7-9 | 3 | 3010 | 60s |
| Wk 2 | 8-10 | 3 | 3010 | 50s |
| Wk 3 | 9-11 | 3 | 3010 | 45s |
| Wk 4 | 10-12 | 2 | 3010 | 40s |
| **D1: Standing Dumbbell Curls** | | | | |
| Wk 1 | 10-12 | 3 | 3010 | 60s |
| Wk 2 | 9-11 | 3 | 3010 | 50s |
| Wk 3 | 8-10 | 3 | 3010 | 45s |
| Wk 4 | 7-9 | 2 | 3010 | 40s |
| **D2: Overhead Triceps Extensions** | | | | |
| Wk 1 | 10-12 | 3 | 3011 | 60s |
| Wk 2 | 9-11 | 3 | 3011 | 50s |
| Wk 3 | 8-10 | 3 | 3011 | 45s |
| Wk 4 | 7-9 | 2 | 3011 | 40 |

## *EA* Football Phase 1: Day 2: Structural Balance

| Week | Reps | Sets | Tempo | Rest |
|------|------|------|-------|------|
| **A1: Box Step Ups** | | | | |
| Wk 1 | 10-12/leg | 3 | 1010 | 60s |
| Wk 2 | 9-11 /leg | 3 | 1010 | 50s |
| Wk 3 | 8-10 /leg | 3 | 1010 | 45s |
| Wk 4 | 7-9/leg | 2 | 1010 | 40s |
| **A2: Dips** | | | | |
| Wk 1 | 7-9 | 3 | 3011 | 60s |
| Wk 2 | 8-10 | 3 | 3011 | 50s |
| Wk 3 | 9-11 | 3 | 3011 | 45s |
| Wk 4 | 10-12 | 2 | 3011 | 40s |
| **B1: Romanian Deadlift** | | | | |
| Wk 1 | 10-12 | 3 | 3010 | 60s |
| Wk 2 | 9-11 | 3 | 3010 | 50s |
| Wk 3 | 8-10 | 3 | 3010 | 45s |
| Wk 4 | 7-9 | 2 | 3010 | 40s |
| **B2: Lat Pulldowns** | | | | |
| Wk 1 | 10-12 | 3 | 3010 | 60s |
| Wk 2 | 9-11 | 3 | 3010 | 50s |
| Wk 3 | 8-10 | 3 | 3010 | 45s |
| Wk 4 | 7-9 | 2 | 3010 | 40s |
| **C1: Standing DB Overhead Press** | | | | |
| Wk 1 | 10-12 | 3 | 2011 | 60s |
| Wk 2 | 9-11 | 3 | 2011 | 50s |
| Wk 3 | 8-10 | 3 | 2011 | 45s |
| Wk 4 | 7-9 | 2 | 2011 | 40s |
| **C2: Supine Windshield Wipers** | | | | |
| Wk 1 | 8-10 | 3 | 3010 | 60s |
| Wk 2 | 8-10 | 3 | 3010 | 50s |
| Wk 3 | 10-12 | 3 | 3010 | 45s |
| Wk 4 | 10-12 | 2 | 3010 | 40s |
| **D1: Seated Hammer Curls** | | | | |
| Wk 1 | 10-12 | 3 | 3010 | 60s |
| Wk 2 | 9-11 | 3 | 3010 | 50s |
| Wk 3 | 8-10 | 3 | 3010 | 45s |
| Wk 4 | 7-9 | 2 | 3010 | 40s |
| **D2: Close Grip Pushups** | | | | |
| Wk 1 | 7-9 | 3 | 3011 | 60s |
| Wk 2 | 8-10 | 3 | 3011 | 50s |
| Wk 3 | 9-11 | 3 | 3011 | 45s |
| Wk 4 | 10-12 | 2 | 3011 | 40s |

# *EA* Football Phase 1: Day 3: Structural Balance

| Week | Reps | Sets | Tempo | Rest |
|------|------|------|-------|------|
| **A1: Walking Lunges** | | | | |
| Wk 1 | 10-12/leg | 3 | 2010 | 60s |
| Wk 2 | 9-11/leg | 3 | 2010 | 50s |
| Wk 3 | 8-10/leg | 3 | 2010 | 45s |
| Wk 4 | 7-9/leg | 2 | 2010 | 40s |
| **A2: Inverted Rows** | | | | |
| Wk 1 | 7-9 | 3 | 3011 | 60s |
| Wk 2 | 8-10 | 3 | 3011 | 50s |
| Wk 3 | 9-11 | 3 | 3011 | 45s |
| Wk 4 | 10-12 | 2 | 3011 | 40s |
| **B1: Bench Supported Hip Thrusts** | | | | |
| Wk 1 | 10-12 | 3 | 3010 | 60s |
| Wk 2 | 9-11 | 3 | 3010 | 50s |
| Wk 3 | 8-10 | 3 | 3010 | 45s |
| Wk 4 | 7-9 | 2 | 3010 | 40s |
| **B2: Flat DB Bench Press** | | | | |
| Wk 1 | 10-12 | 3 | 4010 | 60s |
| Wk 2 | 9-11 | 3 | 4010 | 50s |
| Wk 3 | 8-10 | 3 | 4010 | 45s |
| Wk 4 | 7-9 | 2 | 4010 | 40s |
| **C1: Seated DB Ext Rotator** | | | | |
| Wk 1 | 10-12/arm | 3 | 3010 | 60s |
| Wk 2 | 9-11/arm | 3 | 3010 | 50s |
| Wk 3 | 8-10 /arm | 3 | 3010 | 45s |
| Wk 4 | 7-9/arm | 2 | 3010 | 40s |
| **C2: Reverse Hyperextensions** | | | | |
| Wk 1 | 8-10 | 3 | 4010 | 60s |
| Wk 2 | 8-10 | 3 | 4010 | 50s |
| Wk 3 | 10-12 | 3 | 4010 | 45s |
| Wk 4 | 10-12 | 2 | 4010 | 40s |
| **D1: Standing Barbell Curls** | | | | |
| Wk 1 | 10-12 | 3 | 4010 | 60s |
| Wk 2 | 9-11 | 3 | 4010 | 50s |
| Wk 3 | 8-10 | 3 | 4010 | 45s |
| Wk 4 | 7-9 | 2 | 4010 | 40s |
| **D2: Triceps Pressdowns** | | | | |
| Wk 1 | 7-9 | 3 | 4010 | 60s |
| Wk 2 | 8-10 | 3 | 4010 | 50s |
| Wk 3 | 9-11 | 3 | 4010 | 45s |
| Wk 4 | 10-12 | 2 | 4010 | 40s |

| Dec | Jan | Feb | Mar | Apr | May |
|------|------|------|------|------|------|
| Phase 1 | Phase 2 | Phase 3 | Phase 4 | Phase 5 | Phase 6 |
| Structural Balance | Accum | Intensification | DUP 1: Strength Density 20 Rep | DUP 2: Waveload Strongman Hypertrophy | DUP 3: Str. Density Strongman Supersets |
| Cond: General Activity | Cond: Genera Activit | Cond: **200m Ev:** Sk:30s, L:35s **120yd Shuttle** Sk:28s L: 33s | Cond: **200m Ev:** Sk:29s, L:33s **120yd Shuttle** Sk:27s L: 33s | Cond: **200m Ev:** Sk:27s, L:32s **120yd Shuttle** Sk:26s L: 33s | Cond: **200m Ev:** Sk:26s, L:31s **120yd Shuttle** Sk:25s L: 32s |

| June | July | Aug | Sept | Oct | Nov |
|------|------|------|------|------|------|
| Phase 7 | Phase 8 | Phase 9 | Phase 10 | Phase 11 | Phase 12 |
| Pre-Summer: Structural Balance | Summer 1 2-a-day | Summer 2 2-a-day | In-Season 1 | In-Season 2 | In-Season 3 |
| Cond: Summer Prep | Cond: Summer SAC Phase 1 | Cond: Summer SAC Phase 2 | Cond: Practice | Cond: Practice | Cond: Practice |

# *EA* Sample One-Year Football S&C Program: **PHASE 2**

## Accumulation

### Duration: 4 Weeks
### Frequency: 4x/week

## Optimal Schedule:

| Monday | Tuesday | Wednesday | Thursday | Friday | Saturday | Sunday |
|--------|---------|-----------|----------|--------|----------|--------|
| Accumulation Day 1: Torso | Accumulation Day 2: Legs | Off/recovery methods | Accumulation Day 3: Torso | Accumulation Day 4: Legs | Off/recover methods | Off/recover methods |

## _EA_ Football Phase 2: ACCUMULATION: Day 1: Torso

| Week | Reps | Sets | Tempo | Rest |
|------|------|------|-------|------|
| **A1: Flat Barbell Bench Press** | | | | |
| Wk 1 | 10-12 | 5 | 4010 | 60s |
| Wk 2 | 9-11 | 5 | 4010 | 60s |
| Wk 3 | 8-10 | 5 | 4010 | 60s |
| Wk 4 | 7-9 | 3 | 4010 | 60s |
| **A2: Chin Ups** | | | | |
| Wk 1 | 10-12 | 5 | 4010 | 60s |
| Wk 2 | 9-11 | 5 | 4010 | 60s |
| Wk 3 | 8-10 | 5 | 4010 | 60s |
| Wk 4 | 7-9 | 3 | 4010 | 60s |
| **B1: Dips** | | | | |
| Wk 1 | 10-12 | 4 | 3011 | 60s |
| Wk 2 | 9-11 | 4 | 3011 | 60s |
| Wk 3 | 8-10 | 4 | 3011 | 60s |
| Wk 4 | 7-9 | 2 | 3011 | 60s |
| **B2: 1 Arm Dumbbell Row** | | | | |
| Wk 1 | 10-12 | 4 | 3010 | 60s |
| Wk 2 | 9-11 | 4 | 3010 | 60s |
| Wk 3 | 8-10 | 4 | 3010 | 60s |
| Wk 4 | 7-9 | 2 | 3010 | 60s |
| **C1: Seated Dumbbell External Rotator** | | | | |
| Wk 1 | 12-15 | 3 | 3020 | 60s |
| Wk 2 | 10-12 | 3 | 3020 | 60s |
| Wk 3 | 10-12 | 3 | 3020 | 60s |
| Wk 4 | 8-10 | 1 | 3020 | 60s |
| **C2: Single Arm Trap-3 Lift** | | | | |
| Wk 1 | 12-15 | 3 | 3021 | 60s |
| Wk 2 | 10-12 | 3 | 3021 | 60s |
| Wk 3 | 10-12 | 3 | 3021 | 60s |
| Wk 4 | 8-10 | 1 | 3021 | 60s |

# *EA* Football Phase 2: ACCUMULATION: Day 2: Legs

| Week | Reps | Sets | Tempo | Rest |
|------|------|------|-------|------|
| **A: Power Clean from mid-thigh** | | | | |
| Wk 1 | 4-5 | 5 | X0X0 | 90s |
| Wk 2 | 4-5 | 5 | X0X0 | 90s |
| Wk 3 | 3-5 | 5 | X0X0 | 90s |
| Wk 4 | 3-5 | 3 | X0X0 | 90s |
| **B1: FFE Dumbbell Split Squats** | | | | |
| Wk 1 | 10-12 | 5 | 4010 | 60s |
| Wk 2 | 10-12 | 5 | 4010 | 60s |
| Wk 3 | 9-11 | 5 | 4010 | 60s |
| Wk 4 | 8-10 | 3 | 4010 | 60 |
| **B2: Hamstring Curls (Prone or Swiss Ball)** | | | | |
| Wk 1 | 8-10 | 5 | 3010 | 60s |
| Wk 2 | 8-10 | 5 | 3010 | 60s |
| Wk 3 | 6-8 | 5 | 3010 | 60s |
| Wk 4 | 6-8 | 3 | 3010 | 60s |
| **C: Walking Lunges** | | | | |
| Wk 1 | 10-12/leg | 4 | 2010 | 60s |
| Wk 2 | 10-12/leg | 4 | 2010 | 60s |
| Wk 3 | 8-10 /leg | 4 | 2010 | 60s |
| Wk 4 | 8-10 /leg | 2 | 2010 | 60 |
| **C1: Reverse Hyperextensions** | | | | |
| Wk 1 | 8-10 | 3 | 2022 | 60s |
| Wk 2 | 9-11 | 3 | 2022 | 60s |
| Wk 3 | 10-12 | 3 | 2022 | 60s |
| Wk 4 | 10-12 | 1 | 2022 | 60s |
| **C2: Back Extensions** | | | | |
| Wk 1 | 8-10 | 3 | 2022 | 60s |
| Wk 2 | 9-11 | 3 | 2022 | 60s |
| Wk 3 | 10-12 | 3 | 2022 | 60s |
| Wk 4 | 10-12 | 1 | 2022 | 60s |

## _EA_ Football Phase 2: ACCUMULATION: **Day 3:** Torso

| Week | Reps | Exercise Sets | Tempo | Rest |
|------|------|------|-------|------|
| **A1: Incline Dumbbell Bench Press** | | | | |
| Wk 1 | 10-12 | 5 | 4010 | 60s |
| Wk 2 | 9-11 | 5 | 4010 | 60s |
| Wk 3 | 8-10 | 5 | 4010 | 60s |
| Wk 4 | 7-9 | 3 | 4010 | 60s |
| **A2: Pullup Ups** | | | | |
| Wk 1 | 10-12 | 5 | 4010 | 60s |
| Wk 2 | 9-11 | 5 | 4010 | 60s |
| Wk 3 | 8-10 | 5 | 4010 | 60s |
| Wk 4 | 7-9 | 3 | 4010 | 60s |
| **B1: Weighted Pushup Variation** | | | | |
| Wk 1 | 10-12 | 4 | 3011 | 60s |
| Wk 2 | 9-11 | 4 | 3011 | 60s |
| Wk 3 | 8-10 | 4 | 3011 | 60s |
| Wk 4 | 7-9 | 2 | 3011 | 60s |
| **B2: Inverted Row** | | | | |
| Wk 1 | 10-12 | 4 | 3010 | 60s |
| Wk 2 | 9-11 | 4 | 3010 | 60s |
| Wk 3 | 8-10 | 4 | 3010 | 60s |
| Wk 4 | 7-9 | 2 | 3010 | 60s |
| **C1: Seated Dumbell External Rotator** | | | | |
| Wk 1 | 12-15 | 3 | 3020 | 60s |
| Wk 2 | 10-12 | 3 | 3020 | 60s |
| Wk 3 | 10-12 | 3 | 3020 | 60s |
| Wk 4 | 8-10 | 1 | 3020 | 60s |
| **C2: Trap-3 Lift** | | | | |
| Wk 1 | 12-15 | 3 | 3021 | 60s |
| Wk 2 | 10-12 | 3 | 3021 | 60s |
| Wk 3 | 10-12 | 3 | 3021 | 60s |
| Wk 4 | 8-10 | 1 | 3021 | 60s |

# *EA* Football Phase 2: ACCUMULATION: Day 4: Legs

|  |  | Exercise |  |  |
| --- | --- | --- | --- | --- |
| Week | Reps | Sets | Tempo | Rest |

**A: Power Clean from hang above knee**

| Week | Reps | Sets | Tempo | Rest |
| --- | --- | --- | --- | --- |
| Wk 1 | 5 | 5 | X0X0 | 90s |
| Wk 2 | 4-5 | 5 | X0X0 | 90s |
| Wk 3 | 3-5 | 5 | X0X0 | 90s |
| Wk 4 | 3-5 | 3 | X0X0 | 90s |

**B1: Heels Elevated Back Squats**

| Wk 1 | 10-12 | 5 | 4110 | 60s |
| --- | --- | --- | --- | --- |
| Wk 2 | 10-12 | 5 | 4110 | 60s |
| Wk 3 | 9-11 | 5 | 4110 | 60s |
| Wk 4 | 8-10 | 3 | 4110 | 60s |

**B2: Hamstring Curls (Prone or Swiss Ball)**

| Wk 1 | 8-10 | 5 | 3010 | 60s |
| --- | --- | --- | --- | --- |
| Wk 2 | 8-10 | 5 | 3010 | 60s |
| Wk 3 | 6-8 | 5 | 3010 | 60s |
| Wk 4 | 6-8 | 3 | 3010 | 60s |

**C: Box Step Ups**

| Wk 1 | 10-12/leg | 5 | 4010 | 60s |
| --- | --- | --- | --- | --- |
| Wk 2 | 9-11/leg | 5 | 4010 | 60s |
| Wk 3 | 8-10/leg | 5 | 4010 | 60s |
| Wk 4 | 8-10/leg | 3 | 4010 | 60s |

**C1: Rotational Back Extensions**

| Wk 1 | 8-10 | 3 | 2022 | 60s |
| --- | --- | --- | --- | --- |
| Wk 2 | 9-11 | 3 | 2022 | 60s |
| Wk 3 | 10-12 | 3 | 2022 | 60s |
| Wk 4 | 10-12 | 1 | 2022 | 60s |

**C2: Reverse Hyperextensions**

| Wk 1 | 8-10 | 3 | 2022 | 60s |
| --- | --- | --- | --- | --- |
| Wk 2 | 9-11 | 3 | 2022 | 60s |
| Wk 3 | 10-12 | 3 | 2022 | 60s |
| Wk 4 | 10-12 | 1 | 2022 | 60s |

| Dec | Jan | Feb | Mar | Apr | May |
|---|---|---|---|---|---|
| Phase 1 | Phase 2 | Phase 3 | Phase 4 | Phase 5 | Phase 6 |
| Structural Balance | Accum | Intensification | DUP 1: Strength Density 20 Rep | DUP 2: Waveload Strongman Hypertrophy | DUP 3: Str. Density Strongman Supersets |
| Cond: General Activity | Cond: Genera Activit | Cond: **200m Ev:** **Sk:30s, L:35s** **120yd Shuttle** Sk:28s L: 33s | Cond: **200m Ev:** Sk:29s, L:33s **120yd Shuttle** Sk:27s L: 33s | Cond: **200m Ev:** Sk:27s, L:32s **120yd Shuttle** Sk:26s L: 33s | Cond: **200m Ev:** Sk:26s, L:31s **120yd Shuttle** Sk:25s L: 32s |

| June | July | Aug | Sept | Oct | Nov |
|---|---|---|---|---|---|
| Phase 7 | Phase 8 | Phase 9 | Phase 10 | Phase 11 | Phase 12 |
| Pre-Summer: Structural Balance | Summer 1 2-a-day | Summer 2 2-a-day | In-Season 1 | In-Season 2 | In-Season 3 |
| Cond: Summer Prep | Cond: Summer SAC Phase 1 | Cond: Summer SAC Phase 2 | Cond: Practice | Cond: Practice | Cond: Practice |

# *EA* Sample One-Year Football S&C Program: **PHASE 3**

## Intensification

## **Duration:** 4 Weeks
## **Frequency:** 4x/week

## **Optimal Schedule:**

| Monday | Tuesday | Wednesday | Thursday | Friday | Saturday | Sunday |
|---|---|---|---|---|---|---|
| Intensification Day 1: Torso | Intensification Day 2: Legs | Off/recover methods | Intensification Day 3: Torso | Intensification Day 4: Legs | Off/recover methods | Off/recover methods |

# *EA* Football Phase 3: Intensification: Day 1: Torso

| Week | Reps | Exercise Sets | Tempo | Rest |
|------|------|------|-------|------|
| | | **A1: Barbell Bench Press w/chains** | | |
| Wk 1 | 3 | 8 | 30X0 | 60s |
| Wk 2 | 3 | 8 | 30X0 | 60s |
| Wk 3 | 3 | 8 | 30X0 | 60s |
| Wk 4 | 3 | 4 | 30X0 | 60s |
| | **A2: Chin Ups** | | | |
| Wk 1 | 3 | 8 | 30X0 | 90s |
| Wk 2 | 3 | 8 | 30X0 | 90s |
| Wk 3 | 3 | 8 | 30X0 | 90s |
| Wk 4 | 3 | 4 | 30X0 | 90s |
| | **B1: Dips** | | | |
| Wk 1 | 4-6 | 4 | 3011 | 60s |
| Wk 2 | 4-6 | 4 | 3011 | 60s |
| Wk 3 | 3-5 | 4 | 3011 | 60s |
| Wk 4 | 3-5 | 2 | 3011 | 60s |
| | **B2: Bent Over Barbell Rows** | | | |
| Wk 1 | 6-8 | 4 | 3010 | 60s |
| Wk 2 | 6-8 | 4 | 3010 | 60s |
| Wk 3 | 5-7 | 4 | 3010 | 60s |
| Wk 4 | 5-7 | 2 | 3010 | 60s |
| | **C1: Standing Dumbbell Curls** | | | |
| Wk 1 | 6-8 | 4 | 3010 | 60s |
| Wk 2 | 6-8 | 4 | 3010 | 60s |
| Wk 3 | 5-7 | 4 | 3010 | 60s |
| Wk 4 | 5-7 | 2 | 3010 | 60s |
| | **C2: Triceps Pressdowns** | | | |
| Wk 1 | 6-8 | 4 | 3010 | 60s |
| Wk 2 | 6-8 | 4 | 3010 | 60s |
| Wk 3 | 5-7 | 4 | 3010 | 60s |
| Wk 4 | 5-7 | 2 | 3010 | 60s |

## *EA* Football Phase 3: Intensification: Day 2: Legs

| Week | Reps | Exercise Sets | Tempo | Rest |
|------|------|------|-------|------|
| | | **A: High Pulls from hang above knee** | | |
| Wk 1 | 3-5 | 6 | X0X0 | 180s |
| Wk 2 | 3-4 | 6 | X0X0 | 180s |
| Wk 3 | 2-4 | 6 | X0X0 | 180s |
| Wk 4 | 2-3 | 3 | X0X0 | 180s |
| | | **B1: Back Squat** | | |
| Wk 1 | 4-6 | 5 | 31X0 | 90s |
| Wk 2 | 3-5 | 5 | 31X0 | 90s |
| Wk 3 | 3-4 | 5 | 31X0 | 90s |
| Wk 4 | 2-4 | 3 | 31X0 | 90s |
| | | **B2: Prone Hamstring Curl** | | |
| Wk 1 | 4-6 | 5 | 4010 | 120s |
| Wk 2 | 4-6 | 5 | 4010 | 120s |
| Wk 3 | 4-6 | 5 | 4010 | 120s |
| Wk 4 | 4-6 | 3 | 4010 | 120s |
| | | **C1: Good Mornings** | | |
| Wk 1 | 8-10 | 4 | 3010 | 60s |
| Wk 2 | 8-10 | 4 | 3010 | 60s |
| Wk 3 | 6-8 | 4 | 3010 | 60s |
| Wk 4 | 6-8 | 2 | 3010 | 60s |
| | | **C2: Step Forward Lunges** | | |
| Wk 1 | 5-6/leg | 4 | 2010 | 60s |
| Wk 2 | 5-6/leg | 4 | 2010 | 60s |
| Wk 3 | 5-6/leg | 4 | 2010 | 60s |
| Wk 4 | 5-6/leg | 2 | 2010 | 60s |

# _EA_ Football Phase 3: Intensification: Day 3: Torso

| Week | Reps | Sets | Tempo | Rest |
|---|---|---|---|---|
| | | | Exercise | |
| **A1: Barbell Push Press** | | | | |
| Wk 1 | 4-6 | 5 | 10X1 | 60s |
| Wk 2 | 3-5 | 5 | 10X1 | 60s |
| Wk 3 | 3-5 | 5 | 10X1 | 60s |
| Wk 4 | 2-4 | 2 | 10X1 | 60s |
| **A2: Close Neutral Grip Lat Pulldowns** | | | | |
| Wk 1 | 4-6 | 5 | 3010 | 90s |
| Wk 2 | 4-6 | 5 | 3010 | 90s |
| Wk 3 | 4-6 | 5 | 3010 | 90s |
| Wk 4 | 4-6 | 2 | 3010 | 90s |
| **B1: Flat Neutral Grip DB Bench Press** | | | | |
| Wk 1 | 4-6 | 5 | 30X0 | 60s |
| Wk 2 | 4-6 | 5 | 30X0 | 60s |
| Wk 3 | 3-5 | 5 | 30X0 | 60s |
| Wk 4 | 3-5 | 2 | 30X0 | 60s |
| **B2: 1 Arm DB Rows** | | | | |
| Wk 1 | 6-8 | 5 | 2010 | 90s |
| Wk 2 | 6-8 | 5 | 2010 | 90s |
| Wk 3 | 6-8 | 5 | 2010 | 90s |
| Wk 4 | 6-8 | 2 | 2010 | 90s |
| **C1: Standing Hammer Curls** | | | | |
| Wk 1 | 6-8 | 4 | 3010 | 60s |
| Wk 2 | 6-8 | 4 | 3010 | 60s |
| Wk 3 | 5-7 | 4 | 3010 | 60s |
| Wk 4 | 5-7 | 2 | 3010 | 60s |
| **C2: Nosebreakers w/chains** | | | | |
| Wk 1 | 6-8 | 4 | 3010 | 60s |
| Wk 2 | 6-8 | 4 | 3010 | 60s |
| Wk 3 | 5-7 | 4 | 3010 | 60s |
| Wk | 5-7 | 2 | 3010 | 60s |

## *EA* Football Phase 3: Intensification: Day 4: Legs

| Week | Reps | Exercise Sets | Tempo | Rest |
|------|------|------|-------|------|
| **A: Power Clean from hang above knee** | | | | |
| Wk 1 | 3-5 | 6 | X0X0 | 180s |
| Wk 2 | 2-3 | 6 | X0X0 | 180s |
| Wk 3 | 2-4 | 6 | X0X0 | 180s |
| Wk 4 | 2-3 | 3 | X0X0 | 180s |
| **B: Deadlift** | | | | |
| Wk 1 | 4-6 | 5 | 1010 | 120s |
| Wk 2 | 4-6 | 5 | 1010 | 120s |
| Wk 3 | 3-5 | 5 | 1010 | 120s |
| Wk 4 | 3-5 | 2 | 1010 | 120s |
| **C: FFE Barbell Front Rack Split Squat** | | | | |
| Wk 1 | 6-8 | 5 | 3010 | 60s |
| Wk 2 | 6-8 | 5 | 3010 | 60s |
| Wk 3 | 5-7 | 5 | 3010 | 60s |
| Wk 4 | 4-6 | 2 | 3010 | 60s |
| **B2: Swiss Ball Hamstring Curl** | | | | |
| Wk 1 | 8-10 | 5 | 4010 | 90s |
| Wk 2 | 8-10 | 5 | 4010 | 90s |
| Wk 3 | 10-12 | 5 | 4010 | 90s |
| Wk 4 | 10-12 | 2 | 4010 | 90s |

| Dec | Jan | Feb | Mar | Apr | May |
|---|---|---|---|---|---|
| Phase 1 | Phase 2 | Phase 3 | Phase 4 | Phase 5 | Phase 6 |
| Structural Balance | Accum | Intensification | DUP 1: Strength Density 20 Rep | DUP 2: Waveload Strongman Hypertrophy | DUP 3: Str. Density Strongman Supersets |
| Cond: General Activity | Cond: Genera Activit | Cond: **200m Ev:** Sk:30s, L:35s **120yd Shuttle** Sk:28s L: 33s | Cond: **200m Ev:** Sk:29s, L:33s **120yd Shuttle** Sk:27s L: 33s | Cond: **200m Ev:** Sk:27s, L:32s **120yd Shuttle** Sk:26s L: 33s | Cond: **200m Ev:** Sk:26s, L:31s **120yd Shuttle** Sk:25s L: 32s |

| June | July | Aug | Sept | Oct | Nov |
|---|---|---|---|---|---|
| Phase 7 | Phase 8 | Phase 9 | Phase 10 | Phase 11 | Phase 12 |
| Pre-Summer: Structural Balance | Summer 1 2-a-day | Summer 2 2-a-day | In-Season 1 | In-Season 2 | In-Season 3 |
| Cond: Summer Prep | Cond: Summer SAC Phase 1 | Cond: Summer SAC Phase 2 | Cond: Practice | Cond: Practice | Cond: Practice |

# *EA* Sample One-Year Football S&C Program: **PHASE 4**

# **DUP 1** (daily undulating periodization)

## **Duration:** 4 Weeks
## **Frequency:** 3x/week

## **Optimal Schedule:**

| Monday | Tuesday | Wednesday | Thursday | Friday | Saturday | Sunday |
|---|---|---|---|---|---|---|
| DUP 1 Day !: Strength/Power | Off/recover methods | DUP 1 Day 2 Density | Off/recover methods | DUP 1 Day 3 20 Rep | Off/recover methods | Off/recover methods |

## *EA* Football Phase 4: DUP I: Day 1: Strength and Power

| Week | Reps | Exercise Sets | Tempo | Rest |
|------|------|------|-------|------|
| | **A1: Power Clean from the floor** | | | |
| Wk 1 | 3-5 | 5 | X0X0 | 30s |
| Wk 2 | 3-5 | 5 | X0X0 | 30s |
| Wk 3 | 3-5 | 5 | X0X0 | 30s |
| Wk 4 | 3-5 | 3 | X0X0 | 30s |
| | **A2: Broad Jump** | | | |
| Wk 1 | 3 | 5 | NA | 90s |
| Wk 2 | 3 | 5 | NA | 90s |
| Wk 3 | 4 | 5 | NA | 90s |
| Wk 4 | 4-5 | 3 | NA | 90s |
| | **B1: Front Squat** | | | |
| Wk 1 | 4-6 | 5 | 31X0 | 60s |
| Wk 2 | 3-5 | 5 | 31X0 | 60s |
| Wk 3 | 2-4 | 5 | 31X0 | 60s |
| Wk 4 | 2-3 | 2 | 31X0 | 60s |
| | **B2: Flat Barbell Bench Press** | | | |
| Wk 1 | 4-6 | 5 | 30X0 | 60s |
| Wk 2 | 4-6 | 5 | 30X0 | 60s |
| Wk 3 | 3-5 | 5 | 30X0 | 60s |
| Wk 4 | 3-5 | 2 | 30X0 | 60s |
| | **B3: Glute Ham Raise** | | | |
| Wk 1 | 4-6 | 5 | 3010 | 60s |
| Wk 2 | 4-6 | 5 | 3010 | 60s |
| Wk 3 | 3-5 | 5 | 3010 | 60s |
| Wk 4 | 3-5 | 2 | 3010 | 60s |
| | **B4: Chin-Ups** | | | |
| Wk 1 | 4-6 | 5 | 3010 | 60s |
| Wk 2 | 4-6 | 5 | 3010 | 60s |
| Wk 3 | 3-5 | 5 | 3010 | 60s |
| Wk 4 | 3-5 | 2 | 3010 | 60s |

## *EA* Football Phase 4: DUP I: Day 2: Density

| Week | Reps | Sets | Tempo | Rest |
|------|------|------|-------|------|
| **A1: Flat Dumbbell Bench Press** | | | | |
| Wk 1 | 5-10 | 10mins | 1010 | |
| Wk 2 | 5-10 | 10mins | 1010 | |
| Wk 3 | 5-10 | 10mins | 1010 | |
| Wk 4 | 5-10 | 5mins | 1010 | |
| **A2: Inverted Ring Rows** | | | | |
| Wk 1 | 5-10 | 10mins | 1010 | |
| Wk 2 | 5-10 | 10mins | 1010 | |
| Wk 3 | 5-10 | 10mins | 1010 | |
| Wk 4 | 5-10 | 5mins | 1010 | |
| **B1: Seated DB Curls** | | | | |
| Wk 1 | 5-10 | 10mins | 1010 | |
| Wk 2 | 5-10 | 10mins | 1010 | |
| Wk 3 | 5-10 | 10mins | 1010 | |
| Wk 4 | 5-10 | 5mins | 1010 | |
| **B2: Overhead Cable Triceps Extensions** | | | | |
| Wk 1 | 5-10 | 10mins | 1010 | |
| Wk 2 | 5-10 | 10mins | 1010 | |
| Wk 3 | 5-10 | 10mins | 1010 | |
| Wk 4 | 5-10 | 5mins | 1010 | |
| **C1: Deadlift** | | | | |
| Wk 1 | 10 | 10mins | 1010 | |
| Wk 2 | 10 | 10mins | 1010 | |
| Wk 3 | 10 | 10mins | 1010 | |
| Wk 4 | 10 | 5mins | 1010 | |
| **C2: Step Forward Lunges** | | | | |
| Wk 1 | 20 | 10mins | 1010 | |
| Wk 2 | 20 | 10mins | 1010 | |
| Wk 3 | 20 | 10mins | 1010 | |
| Wk 4 | 20 | 5mins | 1010 | |
| **C3: Seated DB Overhead Press** | | | | |
| Wk 1 | 15 | 10mins | 1010 | |
| Wk 2 | 15 | 10mins | 1010 | |
| Wk 3 | 15 | 10mins | 1010 | |
| Wk 4 | 15 | 5mins | 1010 | |

## *EA* Football Phase 4: DUP I: Day 3: 20 Rep Day

| Week | Reps | Sets | Tempo | Rest |
|------|------|------|-------|------|
| **A1: Deadlift** | | | | |
| Wk 1 | 20 | 3 | 1010 | 60s |
| Wk 2 | 20 | 3 | 1010 | 60s |
| Wk 3 | 20 | 4 | 1010 | 60s |
| Wk 4 | 20 | 2 | 1010 | 60s |
| **A2: Flat Fat Grip BB Bench Press w/chains** | | | | |
| Wk 1 | 20 | 3 | 1010 | 60s |
| Wk 2 | 20 | 3 | 1010 | 60s |
| Wk 3 | 20 | 4 | 1010 | 60s |
| Wk 4 | 20 | 2 | 1010 | **60s** |
| **A3: Chin Up  Supinated Grip Lat Pulldowns** | | | | |
| Wk 1 | 20 | 3 | 1010 | 60s |
| Wk 2 | 20 | 3 | 1010 | 60s |
| Wk 3 | 20 | 4 | 1010 | 60s |
| Wk 4 | 20 | 2 | 1010 | **60s** |
| **A4: Overhead Cable Triceps Extensions** | | | | |
| Wk 1 | 20 | 3 | 1010 | 60s |
| Wk 2 | 20 | 3 | 1010 | 60s |
| Wk 3 | 20 | 4 | 1010 | 60s |
| Wk 4 | 20 | 2 | 1010 | **60s** |
| **A5: Standing DB Curls** | | | | |
| Wk 1 | 20 | 3 | 1010 | 60s |
| Wk 2 | 20 | 3 | 1010 | 60s |
| Wk 3 | 20 | 4 | 1010 | 60s |
| Wk 4 | 20 | 2 | 1010 | 60s |
| **A6: Barbell Back Squats** | | | | |
| Wk 1 | 20 | 3 | 1010 | 60s |
| Wk 2 | 20 | 3 | 1010 | 60s |
| Wk 3 | 20 | 4 | 1010 | 60s |
| Wk 4 | 20 | 2 | 1010 | 120s |

| Dec | Jan | Feb | Mar | Apr | May |
|---|---|---|---|---|---|
| **Phase 1** | Phase 2 | Phase 3 | Phase 4 | Phase 5 | Phase 6 |
| **Structural Balance** | Accum | Intensification | DUP 1: Strength Density 20 Rep | DUP 2: Waveload Strongman Hypertrophy | DUP 3: Str. Density Strongman Supersets |
| **Cond: General Activity** | Cond: General Activit | Cond: **200m Ev:** Sk:30s, L:35s **120yd Shuttle** Sk:28s L: 33s | Cond: **200m Ev:** Sk:29s, L:33s **120yd Shuttle** Sk:27s L: 33s | Cond: **200m Ev:** Sk:27s, L:32s **120yd Shuttle** Sk:26s L: 33s | Cond: **200m Ev:** Sk:26s, L:31s **120yd Shuttle** Sk:25s L: 32s |

| June | July | Aug | Sept | Oct | Nov |
|---|---|---|---|---|---|
| Phase 7 | Phase 8 | Phase 9 | Phase 10 | Phase 11 | Phase 12 |
| Pre-Summer: Structural Balance | Summer 1 2-a-day | Summer 2 2-a-day | In-Season 1 | In-Season 2 | In-Season 3 |
| Cond: Summer Prep | Cond: Summer SAC Phase 1 | Cond: Summer SAC Phase 2 | Cond: Practice | Cond: Practice | Cond: Practice |

# *EA* Sample One-Year Football S&C Program: **PHASE 5**

## DUP 2 (daily undulating periodization)

## Duration: 4 Weeks
## Frequency: 3x/week

## Optimal Schedule:

| Monday | Tuesday | Wednesday | Thursday | Friday | Saturday | Sunday |
|---|---|---|---|---|---|---|
| DUP 2 Day 1: Strength/Power | Off/recover methods | DUP 2 Day 2 Strongman | Off/recover methods | DUP 2 Day 3 Hypertrophy | Off/recover methods | Off/recover methods |

## *EA* Football Phase 5: DUP II: Day 1: Waveloading Strength and Power

| Week | Reps | Exercise Sets | Tempo | Rest |
|------|------|------|-------|------|
| | **A1:  Power Clean from the floor** | | | |
| Wk 1 | 3,2,1,3,2,1 | 6 | X0X0 | 30s |
| Wk 2 | 3,2,1,3,2,1 | 6 | X0X0 | 30s |
| Wk 3 | 3,2,1,3,2,1 | 6 | X0X0 | 30s |
| Wk 4 | 3,2,1, | 3 | X0X0 | 30s |
| | **A2: Broad Jump** | | | |
| Wk 1 | 3 | 6 | NA | 90s |
| Wk 2 | 3 | 6 | NA | 90s |
| Wk 3 | 4 | 6 | NA | 90s |
| Wk 4 | 4-5 | 3 | NA | 90s |
| | **B:  Back Squat** | | | |
| Wk 1 | 5,3,2,5,3,2 | 6 | 31X0 | 90s |
| Wk 2 | 5,3,2,5,3,2 | 6 | 31X0 | 90s |
| Wk 3 | 5,3,2,5,3,2 | 6 | 31X0 | 90s |
| Wk 4 | 5,3,2, | 3 | 31X0 | 90s |
| | **C1: Flat Barbell Bench Press with chains** | | | |
| Wk 1 | 5,3,2,5,3,2 | 6 | 31X0 | 60s |
| Wk 2 | 5,3,2,5,3,2 | 6 | 31X0 | 60s |
| Wk 3 | 5,3,2,5,3,2 | 6 | 31X0 | 60s |
| Wk 4 | 5,3,2, | 3 | 31X0 | 60s |
| | **C2: Chin Ups** | | | |
| Wk 1 | 5,3,2,5,3,2 | 6 | 31X0 | 60s |
| Wk 2 | 5,3,2,5,3,2 | 6 | 31X0 | 60s |
| Wk 3 | 5,3,2,5,3,2 | 6 | 31X0 | 60s |
| Wk 4 | 5,3,2, | 3 | 31X0 | 60s |

# *EA* Football Phase 5: DUP II: Day 2: Strongman

| Week | Reps | Exercise Sets | Tempo | Rest |
|------|------|------|-------|------|
| | | **A1: Tire Flips** | | |
| Wk 1 | 3-5 | 5 | X0X0 | 30s |
| Wk 2 | 3-4 | 5 | X0X0 | 30s |
| Wk 3 | 2-3 | 6 | X0X0 | 30s |
| Wk 4 | 2-3 | 3 | X0X0 | 30s |
| | | **A2: 10-15 yd Prowler Acceleration** | | |
| Wk 1 | 10-15yds | 5 | NA | 60s |
| Wk 2 | 10-15yds | 5 | NA | 60s |
| Wk 3 | 10-15yds | 6 | NA | 60s |
| Wk 4 | 10-15yds | 3 | NA | 60s |
| | | **B1: Overhead Med Ball Throws** | | |
| Wk 1 | 4-6 | 5 | NA | 30s |
| Wk 2 | 4-6 | 5 | NA | 30s |
| Wk 3 | 4-6 | 5 | NA | 30s |
| Wk 4 | 4-6 | 3 | NA | 30s |
| | | **B2: Autoregulated Vertical Jump** | | |
| Wk 1 | 2-5 | 5 | NA | 20s |
| Wk 2 | 2-5 | 5 | NA | 20s |
| Wk 3 | 2-5 | 5 | NA | 20s |
| Wk 4 | 2-5 | 3 | NA | 20s |
| | | **B3: Chest Pass Med Ball Throws** | | |
| Wk 1 | 4-6 | 5 | NA | 60s |
| Wk 2 | 4-6 | 5 | NA | 60s |
| Wk 3 | 4-6 | 5 | NA | 60s |
| Wk 4 | 4-6 | 3 | NA | 60s |
| | | **C1: Farmer Carry/HellBarrow** | | |
| Wk 1 | 20-30yds | 5 | NA | 60s |
| Wk 2 | 20-30yds | 5 | NA | 60s |
| Wk 3 | 20-30yds | 5 | NA | 60s |
| Wk 4 | 20-30yds | 2 | NA | 60s |
| | | **C2: Backward back sled drag** | | |
| Wk 1 | 20-30yds | 5 | NA | 90s |
| Wk 2 | 20-30yds | 5 | NA | 90s |
| Wk 3 | 20-30yds | 5 | NA | 90s |
| Wk 4 | 20-30yds | 2 | NA | 60s |

## *EA* Football Phase 5: DUP II: Day 3: Hypertrophy

| Week | Reps | Sets | Tempo | Rest |
|------|------|------|-------|------|
| **A1: Deadlift** | | | | |
| Wk 1 | 10 | 5 | 2010 | 60s |
| Wk 2 | 10 | 5 | 2010 | 60s |
| Wk 3 | 10 | 5 | 2010 | 60s |
| Wk 4 | 10 | 2 | 2010 | 60s |
| **A2: Incline DB Bench Press** | | | | |
| Wk 1 | 10 | 5 | 4010 | 30s |
| Wk 2 | 10 | 5 | 4010 | 30s |
| Wk 3 | 10 | 5 | 4010 | 30s |
| Wk 4 | 10 | 2 | 4010 | 30s |
| **A3: Step Forward Lunges** | | | | |
| Wk 1 | 10/leg | 5 | 2010 | 30s |
| Wk 2 | 10/leg | 5 | 2010 | 30s |
| Wk 3 | 10/leg | 5 | 2010 | 30s |
| Wk 4 | 10/leg | 2 | 2010 | 30s |
| **A4: Pull Ups** | | | | |
| Wk 1 | 10 | 5 | 4010 | 30s |
| Wk 2 | 10 | 5 | 4010 | 30s |
| Wk 3 | 10 | 5 | 4010 | 30s |
| Wk 4 | 10 | 2 | 4010 | 180s |
| **B1: Standing Barbell Curls** | | | | |
| Wk 1 | 10 | 3 | 3010 | 60s |
| Wk 2 | 10 | 3 | 3010 | 60s |
| Wk 3 | 10 | 3 | 3010 | 60s |
| Wk 4 | 10 | 1 | 3010 | 60s |
| **B2: Overhead DB Triceps Extensions** | | | | |
| Wk 1 | 10 | 3 | 3010 | 60s |
| Wk 2 | 10 | 3 | 3010 | 60s |
| Wk 3 | 10 | 3 | 3010 | 60s |
| Wk 4 | 10 | 1 | 3010 | 60s |

| Dec | Jan | Feb | Mar | Apr | May |
|---|---|---|---|---|---|
| Phase 1 | Phase 2 | Phase 3 | Phase 4 | Phase 5 | Phase 6 |
| Structural Balance | Accum | Intensification | DUP 1: Strength Density 20 Rep | DUP 2: Waveload Strongman Hypertrophy | DUP 3: Str. Density Strongman Supersets |
| Cond: General Activity | Cond: Genera Activit | Cond: **200m Ev:** Sk:30s, L:35s **120yd Shuttle** Sk:28s L: 33s | Cond: **200m Ev:** Sk:29s, L:33s **120yd Shuttle** Sk:27s L: 33s | Cond: **200m Ev:** Sk:27s, L:32s **120yd Shuttle** Sk:26s L: 33s | Cond: **200m Ev:** Sk:26s, L:31s **120yd Shuttle** Sk:25s L: 32s |

| June | July | Aug | Sept | Oct | Nov |
|---|---|---|---|---|---|
| Phase 7 | Phase 8 | Phase 9 | Phase 10 | Phase 11 | Phase 12 |
| Pre-Summer: Structural Balance | Summer 1 2-a-day | Summer 2 2-a-day | In-Season 1 | In-Season 2 | In-Season 3 |
| Cond: Summer Prep | Cond: Summer SAC Phase 1 | Cond: Summer SAC Phase 2 | Cond: Practice | Cond: Practice | Cond: Practice |

# *EA* Sample One-Year Football S&C Program: **PHASE 6**

## DUP 3 (daily undulating periodization)

## Duration: 4 Weeks
## Frequency: 3x/week

## Optimal Schedule:

| Monday | Tuesday | Wednesday | Thursday | Friday | Saturday | Sunday |
|---|---|---|---|---|---|---|
| DUP 3 Day I: Strength Density | Off/recover methods | DUP 3 Day 2 Strongman | Off/recover methods | DUP 3 Day 3 Superset Hyp | Off/recover methods | Off/recover methods |

167

## *EA* Football Phase 6: DUP III: Day 1:
Strength Density

| Week | Reps | Exercise Sets | Tempo | Rest |
|------|------|------|-------|------|
| | **A: Power Clean from the floor** | | | |
| Wk 1 | 1-5(Goal 50) | 10mins | X0X0 | NA |
| Wk 2 | 1-5(Goal 50) | 10mins | X0X0 | NA |
| Wk 3 | 1-5(Goal 50) | 10mins | X0X0 | NA |
| Wk 4 | 1-5(Goal 50) | 5mins | X0X0 | NA |
| | **B: Back Squat (Teams of 3)** | | | |
| Wk 1 | 3(goal 48-60)20mins | | NA | NA |
| Wk 2 | 3(goal 48-60)20mins | | NA | NA |
| Wk 3 | 3(goal 48-60)20mins | | NA | NA |
| Wk 4 | 3(goal 48-60)10mins | | NA | NA |
| | **C1: Flat Barbell Bench Press (Teams of 3)** | | | |
| Wk 1 | 3(goal 30-45)20mins | | NA | NA |
| Wk 2 | 3(goal 30-45)20mins | | NA | NA |
| Wk 3 | 3(goal 30-45)20mins | | NA | NA |
| Wk 4 | 3(goal 30-45)10mins | | NA | NA |
| | **C2: Chin Ups (Teams of 3)** | | | |
| Wk 1 | 3(goal 30-45)20mins | | NA | NA |
| Wk 2 | 3(goal 30-45)20mins | | NA | NA |
| Wk 3 | 3(goal 30-45)20mins | | NA | NA |
| Wk 4 | 3(goal 30-45)10mins | | NA | NA |

# *EA* Football Phase 6: DUP III: Day 2: Strongman

|       |                | Exercise |       |       |
|-------|----------------|----------|-------|-------|
| Week  | Reps           | Sets     | Tempo | Rest  |
| **A1/A2: Tire Flip/Sled Drag Sequence** | | | | |
| Wk 1  | 2/drag/2/drag 10 | | X0X0 | 120s |
| Wk 2  | 2/drag/2/drag 10 | | X0X0 | 120s |
| Wk 3  | 2/drag/2/drag 10 | | X0X0 | 120s |
| Wk 4  | 2/drag/2/drag 5  | | X0X0 | 120s |
| **B1: Barbell/Super Yoke Carry** | | | | |
| Wk 1  | 10-20yds       | 5        | NA    | 30s   |
| Wk 2  | 10-20yds       | 5        | NA    | 30s   |
| Wk 3  | 10-20yds       | 6        | NA    | 30s   |
| Wk 4  | 10-20yds       | 3        | NA    | 30s   |
| **B2: Farmer Carry** | | | | |
| Wk 1  | 10-20yds       | 5        | NA    | 90s   |
| Wk 2  | 10-20yds       | 5        | NA    | 90s   |
| Wk 3  | 10-20yds       | 6        | NA    | 90s   |
| Wk 4  | 10-20yds       | 3        | NA    | 90s   |
| **C1: Prowler Push** | | | | |
| Wk 1  | 20-30yds       | 5        | NA    | 30s   |
| Wk 2  | 20-30yds       | 5        | NA    | 30s   |
| Wk 3  | 20-30yds       | 5        | NA    | 30s   |
| Wk 4  | 20-30yds       | 2        | NA    | 30s   |
| **C2: Hand Over Hand Rope Pull** | | | | |
| Wk 1  | 20-30yds       | 5        | NA    | 90s   |
| Wk 2  | 20-30yds       | 5        | NA    | 90s   |
| Wk 3  | 20-30yds       | 5        | NA    | 90s   |
| Wk 4  | 20-30yds       | 2        | NA    | 60s   |

# _EA_ Football Phase 6: DUP III: Day 3: Hypertrophy

| Week | Reps | Sets | Tempo | Rest |
|------|------|------|-------|------|
| | **A1:  Dips** | | | |
| Wk 1 | 8-10 | 4 | 3011 | 20s |
| Wk 2 | 8-10 | 4 | 3011 | 20s |
| Wk 3 | 8-10 | 4 | 3011 | 20s |
| Wk 4 | 8-10 | 2 | 3011 | 20s |
| | **A2: Flat DB Bench Press** | | | |
| Wk 1 | 8-10 | 4 | 4010 | 60s |
| Wk 2 | 8-10 | 4 | 4010 | 60s |
| Wk 3 | 8-10 | 4 | 4010 | 60s |
| Wk 4 | 8-10 | 2 | 4010 | 60s |
| | **A3:  Close Neutral Grip Chin Ups** | | | |
| Wk 1 | 8-10 | 4 | 3010 | 20s |
| Wk 2 | 8-10 | 4 | 3010 | 20s |
| Wk 3 | 8-10 | 4 | 3010 | 20s |
| Wk 4 | 8-10 | 2 | 3010 | 20s |
| | **A4: Bent Over Barbell Rows** | | | |
| Wk 1 | 8-10 | 4 | 3011 | 60s |
| Wk 2 | 8-10 | 4 | 3011 | 60s |
| Wk 3 | 8-10 | 4 | 3011 | 60s |
| Wk 4 | 8-10 | 2 | 3011 | 60s |
| | **B1: Front Squat** | | | |
| Wk 1 | 5-6 | 4 | 31X0 | 30s |
| Wk 2 | 5-6 | 4 | 31X0 | 30s |
| Wk 3 | 5-6 | 4 | 31X0 | 30s |
| Wk 4 | 5-6 | 2 | 31X0 | 30s |
| | **B2: Hamstring Curls** | | | |
| Wk 1 | 6-8 | 4 | 3010 | 30s |
| Wk 2 | 6-8 | 4 | 3010 | 30s |
| Wk 3 | 6-8 | 4 | 3010 | 30s |
| Wk 4 | 6-8 | 2 | 3010 | 30s |
| | **B3: Walking Lunges** | | | |
| Wk 1 | 20-24 | 4 | 2010 | 90s |
| Wk 2 | 20-24 | 4 | 2010 | 90s |
| Wk 3 | 20-24 | 4 | 2010 | 90s |
| Wk 4 | 20-24 | 2 | 2010 | 90s |

| Dec | Jan | Feb | Mar | Apr | May |
|---|---|---|---|---|---|
| Phase 1 | Phase 2 | Phase 3 | Phase 4 | Phase 5 | Phase 6 |
| Structural Balance | Accum | Intensification | DUP 1: Strength Density 20 Rep | DUP 2: Waveload Strongman Hypertrophy | DUP 3: Str. Density Strongman Supersets |
| Cond: General Activity | Cond: Genera Activit | Cond: **200m Ev:** Sk:30s, L:35s **120yd Shuttle** Sk:28s L: 33s | Cond: **200m Ev:** Sk:29s, L:33s **120yd Shuttle** Sk:27s L: 33s | Cond: **200m Ev:** Sk:27s, L:32s **120yd Shuttle** Sk:26s L: 33s | Cond: **200m Ev:** Sk:26s, L:31s **120yd Shuttle** Sk:25s L: 32s |

| June | July | Aug | Sept | Oct | Nov |
|---|---|---|---|---|---|
| Phase 7 | Phase 8 | Phase 9 | Phase 10 | Phase 11 | Phase 12 |
| Pre-Summer: Structural Balance | Summer 1 2-a-day | Summer 2 2-a-day | In-Season 1 | In-Season 2 | In-Season 3 |
| Cond: Summer Prep | Cond: Summer SAC Phase 1 | Cond: Summer SAC Phase 2 | Cond: Practice | Cond: Practice | Cond: Practice |

# *EA* Sample One-Year Football S&C Program: **PHASE 7**

# Pre-Summer Structural Balance

## Duration: 2 Weeks
## Frequency: 2x/week

| Monday | Tuesday | Wednesday | Thursday | Friday | Saturday | Sunday |
|---|---|---|---|---|---|---|
| Pre-Summer Day 1 Structural Balance | Off/recover methods | Off/recover methods | Pre-Summer Day 2: Structural Balance | Off/recover methods | Off/recover methods | Off/recover methods |

## _EA_ Football Phase 7: Day 1: Pre-Summer Structural Balance/Recovery

| Week | Reps | Sets | Tempo | Rest |
|------|------|------|-------|------|
| | **A1: FFE Dumbbell Split Squats** | | | |
| Wk 1 | 10-12/leg | 3 | 4010 | 60s |
| Wk 2 | 8-10/leg | 2 | 4010 | 60s |
| | **A2: Chin Ups** | | | |
| Wk 1 | 10-12 | 3 | 3010 | 60s |
| Wk 2 | 8-10 | 2 | 3010 | 60s |
| | **B1: Swiss Ball Hamstring Curls** | | | |
| Wk 1 | 10-12 | 3 | 4010 | 60s |
| Wk 2 | 10-12 | 2 | 4010 | 50s |
| | **B2: Incline Dumbbell Bench Press** | | | |
| Wk 1 | 10-12 | 3 | 4010 | 60s |
| Wk 2 | 8-10 | 2 | 4010 | 50s |
| | **C1: Upright Rows** | | | |
| Wk 1 | 10-12 | 3 | 2010 | 60s |
| Wk 2 | 8-10 | 2 | 2010 | 50s |
| | **C2: Low Back Extensions** | | | |
| Wk 1 | 10-12 | 3 | 3010 | 60s |
| Wk 2 | 10-12 | 2 | 3010 | 50s |
| | **D1: Standing Dumbbell Curls** | | | |
| Wk 1 | 10-12 | 3 | 3010 | 60s |
| Wk 2 | 8-10 | 2 | 3010 | 50s |
| | **D2: Overhead Triceps Extensions** | | | |
| Wk 1 | 10-12 | 3 | 3011 | 60s |
| Wk 2 | 8-10 | 2 | 3011 | 50s |

### *EA* Football Phase 7: Day 1: Pre-Summer Structural Balance/Recovery

| Week | Reps | Sets | Tempo | Rest |
|------|------|------|-------|------|
| **A1: Box Step Ups** | | | | |
| Wk 1 | 10-12/leg | 3 | 1010 | 60s |
| Wk 2 | 8-10/leg | 2 | 1010 | 60s |
| **A2: Dips** | | | | |
| Wk 1 | 10-12 | 3 | 3011 | 60s |
| Wk 2 | 8-10 | 2 | 3011 | 60s |
| **B1: Romanian Deadlift** | | | | |
| Wk 1 | 10-12 | 3 | 3010 | 60s |
| Wk 2 | 8-10 | 2 | 3010 | 50s |
| **B2: Lat Pulldowns** | | | | |
| Wk 1 | 10-12 | 3 | 3010 | 60s |
| Wk 2 | 8-10 | 2 | 3010 | 50s |
| **C1: Standing DB Overhead Press** | | | | |
| Wk 1 | 10-12 | 3 | 2011 | 60s |
| Wk 2 | 8-10 | 2 | 2011 | 50s |
| **C2: Supine Windshield Wipers** | | | | |
| Wk 1 | 10-12 | 3 | 3010 | 60s |
| Wk 2 | 10-12 | 2 | 3010 | 50s |
| **D1: Seated Hammer Curls** | | | | |
| Wk 1 | 10-12 | 3 | 3010 | 60s |
| Wk 2 | 8-10 | 2 | 3010 | 50s |
| **D2: Close Grip Pushups** | | | | |
| Wk 1 | 10-12 | 3 | 3011 | 60s |
| Wk 2 | 8-10 | 2 | 3011 | 50s |

| Dec | Jan | Feb | Mar | Apr | May |
|---|---|---|---|---|---|
| Phase 1 | Phase 2 | Phase 3 | Phase 4 | Phase 5 | Phase 6 |
| Structural Balance | Accum | Intensification | DUP 1: Strength Density 20 Rep | DUP 2: Waveload Strongman Hypertrophy | DUP 3: Str. Density Strongman Supersets |
| Cond: General Activity | Cond: Genera Activit | Cond: **200m Ev:** Sk:30s, L:35s **120yd Shuttle** Sk:28s L: 33s | Cond: **200m Ev:** Sk:29s, L:33s **120yd Shuttle** Sk:27s L: 33s | Cond: **200m Ev:** Sk:27s, L:32s **120yd Shuttle** Sk:26s L: 33s | Cond: **200m Ev:** Sk:26s, L:31s **120yd Shuttle** Sk:25s L: 32s |

| June | July | Aug | Sept | Oct | Nov |
|---|---|---|---|---|---|
| Phase 7 | Phase 8 | Phase 9 | Phase 10 | Phase 11 | Phase 12 |
| Pre-Summer: Structural Balance | Summer 1 2-a-day | Summer 2 2-a-day | In-Season 1 | In-Season 2 | In-Season 3 |
| Cond: Summer Prep | Cond: Summer SAC Phase 1 | Cond: Summer SAC Phase 2 | Cond: Practice | Cond: Practice | Cond: Practice |

# *EA* Sample One-Year Football S&C Program: **PHASE 8**

## Summer 2-a-Day I

## Duration: 4 Weeks
## Frequency: 8x/week

| Monday | Tuesday | Wednesday | Thursday | Friday | Saturday | Sunday |
|---|---|---|---|---|---|---|
| Summer Phase 1 Day 1: AM | Summer Phase 1 Day 2: AM | Off/recover methods | Summer Phase 1 Day 3:AM | Summer Phase 1 Day 4: AM | Off/recover methods | Off/recover methods |
| Summer Phase 1 Day 1: PM | Summer Phase 1 Day 2: PM | | Summer Phase 1 Day 3: PM | Summer Phase 1 Day 4: PM | | |

## *EA* Football Phase 8 Summer 2-a-day: Day 1: AM
**Workout:** Lower Body Strength and Power *(Can substitute with lower body French Contrast program)*

| Week | Reps | Exercise<br>Sets | Tempo | Rest |
|------|------|------|-------|------|
| **A1: Power Clean from the hang above knee** | | | | |
| Wk 1 | 3-5 | 5 | X0X0 | 30s |
| Wk 2 | 3-5 | 5 | X0X0 | 30s |
| Wk 3 | 2-4 | 6 | X0X0 | 30s |
| Wk 4 | 2-4 | 3 | X0X0 | 30s |
| **A2: Depth Drops** | | | | |
| Wk 1 | 3-4 | 5 | NA | 60s |
| Wk 2 | 3-4 | 5 | NA | 60s |
| Wk 3 | 3-4 | 6 | NA | 60s |
| Wk 4 | 3-4 | 3 | NA | 60s |
| **B1: Back Squat with Chains** | | | | |
| Wk 1 | 4-6 | 5 | 30X1 | 30s |
| Wk 2 | 3-5 | 5 | 30X1 | 30s |
| Wk 3 | 3-5 | 5 | 30X1 | 30s |
| Wk 4 | 2-4 | 3 | 30X1 | 30s |
| **B2: Broad Jump** | | | | |
| Wk 1 | 3-4 | 5 | NA | 30s |
| Wk 2 | 3-4 | 5 | NA | 30s |
| Wk 3 | 3-4 | 5 | NA | 30s |
| Wk 4 | 3-4 | 3 | NA | 30s |
| **B3: Swiss Ball or Kneeling Hamstring Curls** | | | | |
| Wk 1 | 10-12 | 5 | 3010 | 60s |
| Wk 2 | 8-10 | 5 | 3010 | 60s |
| Wk 3 | 8-10 | 5 | 3010 | 60s |
| Wk 4 | 8-10 | 3 | 3010 | 60s |
| **C1: Walking Lunges** | | | | |
| Wk 1 | 16-20 | 3 | 20X0 | 90s |
| Wk 2 | 16-20 | 3 | 20X0 | 90s |
| Wk 3 | 16-20 | 3 | 20X0 | 90s |
| Wk 4 | 16-20 | 1 | 20X0 | 90s |

### *EA* Football Phase 8 Summer 2-a-day: Day 1: PM
### Workout: Lower Body Strongman

| Week | Reps | Exercise Sets | Tempo | Rest |
|------|------|------|-------|------|
| **A1: Tire Flips** | | | | |
| Wk 1 | 3-5 | 5 | X0X0 | 30s |
| Wk 2 | 3-4 | 5 | X0X0 | 30s |
| Wk 3 | 2-3 | 6 | X0X0 | 30s |
| Wk 4 | 2-3 | 3 | X0X0 | 30s |
| **A2: 10-15 yd Prowler Acceleration** | | | | |
| Wk 1 | 10-15yds | 5 | NA | 60s |
| Wk 2 | 10-15yds | 5 | NA | 60s |
| Wk 3 | 10-15yds | 5 | NA | 60s |
| Wk 4 | 10-15yds | 3 | NA | 60s |
| **B1: Overhead Med Ball Throws** | | | | |
| Wk 1 | 4-6 | 5 | NA | 30s |
| Wk 2 | 4-6 | 5 | NA | 30s |
| Wk 3 | 4-6 | 5 | NA | 30s |
| Wk 4 | 4-6 | 3 | NA | 30s |
| **B2: Split Jumps** | | | | |
| Wk 1 | 3-4/leg | 5 | NA | 30s |
| Wk 2 | 3-4/leg | 5 | NA | 30s |
| Wk 3 | 3-4/leg | 5 | NA | 30s |
| Wk 4 | 3-4/leg | 3 | NA | 30s |
| **B3: Farmer Carry/HellBarrow** | | | | |
| Wk 1 | 20-30yds | 5 | NA | 60s |
| Wk 2 | 20-30yds | 5 | NA | 60s |
| Wk 3 | 20-30yds | 5 | NA | 60s |
| Wk 4 | 20-30yds | 2 | NA | 60s |
| **C1: Forward down/backward back sled drag** | | | | |
| Wk 1 | 20-30yds | 5 | NA | 90s |
| Wk 2 | 20-30yds | 5 | NA | 90s |
| Wk 3 | 20-30yds | 5 | NA | 90s |
| Wk 4 | 20-30yds | 2 | NA | 60s |

## *EA* Football Phase 8 Summer 2-a-day: Day 2: AM

**Workout:** Upper Body Strength and Power *(Can substitute with upper body French Contrast Program)*

| Week | Reps | Sets | Tempo | Rest |
|------|------|------|-------|------|
| **A1: Flat Barbell Bench Press w/chains** | | | | |
| Wk 1 | 3-5 | 5 | 30X1 | 30s |
| Wk 2 | 3-4 | 5 | 30X1 | 30s |
| Wk 3 | 2-3 | 6 | 30X1 | 30s |
| Wk 4 | 2-3 | 3 | 30X1 | 30s |
| **A2: Jump or clap pushups** | | | | |
| Wk 1 | 3-4 | 5 | NA | 60s |
| Wk 2 | 3-4 | 5 | NA | 60s |
| Wk 3 | 3-4 | 6 | NA | 60s |
| Wk 4 | 3-4 | 3 | NA | 60s |
| **A3: Chin Ups** | | | | |
| Wk 1 | 4-6 | 5 | 30X1 | 30s |
| Wk 2 | 3-5 | 5 | 30X1 | 30s |
| Wk 3 | 2-4 | 6 | 30X1 | 30s |
| Wk 4 | 2-4 | 3 | 30X1 | 30s |
| **A4: Med Ball Slamdowns** | | | | |
| Wk 1 | 6-8 | 5 | NA | 30s |
| Wk 2 | 6-8 | 5 | NA | 30s |
| Wk 3 | 6-8 | 6 | NA | 30s |
| Wk 4 | 6-8 | 3 | NA | 30s |
| **B1: Dips** | | | | |
| Wk 1 | 4-6 | 5 | 3010 | 60s |
| Wk 2 | 4-6 | 5 | 3010 | 60s |
| Wk 3 | 3-5 | 5 | 3010 | 60s |
| Wk 4 | 3-5 | 2 | 3010 | 60s |
| **B2: 1 Arm Dumbbell Rows** | | | | |
| Wk 1 | 4-6 | 5 | 3010 | 60s |
| Wk 2 | 4-6 | 5 | 3010 | 60s |
| Wk 3 | 4-6 | 5 | 3010 | 60s |
| Wk 4 | 4-6 | 2 | 3010 | 60s |

## *EA* Football Phase 8 Summer 2-a-day: Day 2: PM
**Workout:** Upper Body Strongman

| Week | Reps | Sets | Tempo | Rest |
|------|------|------|-------|------|
| **A1: Hand Over Hand Rope Pull** | | | | |
| Wk 1 | 1-2 | 5 | NA | 30s |
| Wk 2 | 1-2 | 5 | NA | 30s |
| Wk 3 | 1-2 | 6 | NA | 30s |
| Wk 4 | 1-2 | 3 | NA | 30s |
| **A2: Overhead Plate or Barbell Carry** | | | | |
| Wk 1 | 20-40yds | 5 | NA | 60s |
| Wk 2 | 20-40yds | 5 | NA | 60s |
| Wk 3 | 20-40yds | 5 | NA | 60s |
| Wk 4 | 20-40yds | 3 | NA | 60s |
| **B1: Hand Over Hand Atlas Stone Slalom Push** | | | | |
| Wk 1 | 20-40yds | 5 | NA | 30s |
| Wk 2 | 20-40yds | 5 | NA | 30s |
| Wk 3 | 20-40yds | 5 | NA | 30s |
| Wk 4 | 20-40yds | 3 | NA | 30s |
| **B2: Sledgehammer Sand or Tire Hits** | | | | |
| Wk 1 | 20 | 5 | NA | 60s |
| Wk 2 | 20 | 5 | NA | 60s |
| Wk 3 | 20 | 5 | NA | 60s |
| Wk 4 | 20 | 3 | NA | 60s |
| **C: Burpees for Height** | | | | |
| Wk 1 | 10 | 5 | NA | 60s |
| Wk 2 | 10 | 5 | NA | 60s |
| Wk 3 | 10 | 5 | NA | 60s |
| Wk 4 | 10 | 2 | NA | 60s |

## *EA* Football Phase 8 Summer 2-a-day: Day 3: AM
**Workout:** Lower Body Strength and Power *(Can substitute with lower body French Contrast Program)*

| Week | Reps | Sets | Exercise Tempo | Rest |
|------|------|------|-------|------|
| **A1: High Pull to Deadlift (Sets 1-3HP/Sets4-6DL)** | | | | |
| Wk 1 | 3-5 | 6 | X0X0 | 30s |
| Wk 2 | 3-4 | 6 | X0X0 | 30s |
| Wk 3 | 2-3 | 6 | X0X0 | 30s |
| Wk 4 | 2-3 | 3 | X0X0 | 30s |
| **A2: Depth Jumps** | | | | |
| Wk 1 | 3-4 | 6 | NA | 60s |
| Wk 2 | 3-4 | 6 | NA | 60s |
| Wk 3 | 3-4 | 6 | NA | 60s |
| Wk 4 | 3-4 | 3 | NA | 60s |
| **B1: Front Squat** | | | | |
| Wk 1 | 4-6 | 5 | 30X1 | 30s |
| Wk 2 | 3-5 | 5 | 30X1 | 30s |
| Wk 3 | 2-4 | 5 | 30X1 | 30s |
| Wk 4 | 2-4 | 3 | 30X1 | 30s |
| **B2: Box Drop 5-10-5** | | | | |
| Wk 1 | 1-2 | 5 | NA | 30s |
| Wk 2 | 1-2 | 5 | NA | 30s |
| Wk 3 | 1-2 | 5 | NA | 30s |
| Wk 4 | 1-2 | 3 | NA | 30s |
| **C1: Glute Ham Raise** | | | | |
| Wk 1 | 6-8 | 5 | 3010 | 60s |
| Wk 2 | 5-7 | 5 | 3010 | 60s |
| Wk 3 | 4-6 | 5 | 3010 | 60s |
| Wk 4 | 4-6 | 2 | 3010 | 60s |
| **C2: Alternating Step Forward Lunges** | | | | |
| Wk 1 | 16-20 | 3 | 20X0 | 90s |
| Wk 2 | 16-20 | 3 | 20X0 | 90s |
| Wk 3 | 16-20 | 3 | 20X0 | 90s |
| Wk 4 | 16-20 | 2 | 20X0 | 90s |

## *EA* Football Phase 8 Summer 2-a-day: Day 3: PM
## Workout: Lower Body Hypertrophy 6-12-24

| Week | Reps | Exercise Sets | Tempo | Rest |
|------|------|------|-------|------|
| | | **A1: Barbell Back Squat** | | |
| Wk 1 | 6 | 5 | 30X1 | 20s |
| Wk 2 | 6 | 5 | 30X1 | 20s |
| Wk 3 | 6 | 5 | 30X1 | 20s |
| Wk 4 | 6 | 2 | 30X1 | 20s |
| | | **A2: Box Step Ups** | | |
| Wk 1 | 12 | 5 | NA | 20s |
| Wk 2 | 12 | 5 | NA | 20s |
| Wk 3 | 12 | 6 | NA | 20s |
| Wk 4 | 12 | 2 | NA | 20s |
| | | **A3: Leg Press or Walking Lunges** | | |
| Wk 1 | 24 | 5 | 20X1 | 120s |
| Wk 2 | 24 | 5 | 20X1 | 120s |
| Wk 3 | 24 | 5 | 20X1 | 120s |
| Wk 4 | 24 | 2 | 20X1 | 120s |

## *EA* Football Phase 8 Summer 2-a-day: Day 4: AM Workout: Upper Body Strength and Power

| Week | Reps | Sets | Tempo | Rest |
|------|------|------|-------|------|
| **A1: Push Press or Jerk** | | | | |
| Wk 1 | 3-5 | 5 | 10X1 | 30s |
| Wk 2 | 3-4 | 5 | 10X1 | 30s |
| Wk 3 | 2-3 | 6 | 10X1 | 30s |
| Wk 4 | 2-3 | 3 | 10X1 | 30s |
| **B1: Pull-ups** | | | | |
| Wk 1 | 4-6 | 5 | 30X1 | 30s |
| Wk 2 | 3-5 | 5 | 30X1 | 30s |
| Wk 3 | 2-4 | 6 | 30X1 | 30s |
| Wk 4 | 2-4 | 3 | 30X1 | 30s |
| **B2: Chest Pass Med Ball Throws** | | | | |
| Wk 1 | 3-4 | 5 | NA | 60s |
| Wk 2 | 3-4 | 5 | NA | 60s |
| Wk 3 | 3-4 | 6 | NA | 60s |
| Wk 4 | 3-4 | 3 | NA | 60s |
| **B3: Pull-ups** | | | | |
| Wk 1 | 4-6 | 5 | 30X1 | 30s |
| Wk 2 | 3-5 | 5 | 30X1 | 30s |
| Wk 3 | 2-4 | 6 | 30X1 | 30s |
| Wk 4 | 2-4 | 3 | 30X1 | 30s |
| **B4: Power Sled Pull Throughs** | | | | |
| Wk 1 | 6-8 | 5 | NA | 30s |
| Wk 2 | 6-8 | 5 | NA | 30s |
| Wk 3 | 6-8 | 6 | NA | 30s |
| Wk 4 | 6-8 | 3 | NA | 30s |
| **C1: Dips** | | | | |
| Wk 1 | 4-6 | 5 | 3010 | 60s |
| Wk 2 | 3-5 | 5 | 3010 | 60s |
| Wk 3 | 3-5 | 5 | 3010 | 60s |
| Wk 4 | 3-5 | 3 | 3010 | 60s |
| **C2: Seated Cable Rows** | | | | |
| Wk 1 | 4-6 | 5 | 3010 | 60s |
| Wk 2 | 4-6 | 5 | 3010 | 60s |
| Wk 3 | 4-6 | 5 | 3010 | 60s |
| Wk 4 | 4-6 | 3 | 3010 | 60s |

### *EA* Football Phase 8 Summer 2-a-day: Day 4: PM
### Workout: Upper Body 6 12 24

| Week | Reps | Sets | Tempo | Rest |
|------|------|------|-------|------|
| **A1:  Dips** | | | | |
| Wk 1 | 6 | 5 | 30X1 | 20s |
| Wk 2 | 6 | 5 | 30X1 | 20s |
| Wk 3 | 6 | 5 | 30X1 | 20s |
| Wk 4 | 6 | 3 | 30X1 | 20s |
| **A2: Flat Barbell Bench Press** | | | | |
| Wk 1 | 12 | 5 | NA | 20s |
| Wk 2 | 12 | 5 | NA | 20s |
| Wk 3 | 12 | 6 | NA | 20s |
| Wk 4 | 12 | 3 | NA | 20s |
| **A3:  Pushups** | | | | |
| Wk 1 | 24 | 5 | 20X1 | 60s |
| Wk 2 | 24 | 5 | 20X1 | 60s |
| Wk 3 | 24 | 5 | 20X1 | 60s |
| Wk 4 | 24 | 3 | 20X1 | 60s |
| **A4:  Close Neutral Grip Chin Ups** | | | | |
| Wk 1 | 6 | 5 | 30X1 | 20s |
| Wk 2 | 6 | 5 | 30X1 | 20s |
| Wk 3 | 6 | 5 | 30X1 | 20s |
| Wk 4 | 6 | 3 | 30X1 | 20s |
| **A5: Seated Cable Reach and Rows** | | | | |
| Wk 1 | 12 | 5 | NA | 20s |
| Wk 2 | 12 | 5 | NA | 20s |
| Wk 3 | 12 | 6 | NA | 20s |
| Wk 4 | 12 | 3 | NA | 20s |
| **A6:  Close Supinated Grip Lat Pulldowns** | | | | |
| Wk 1 | 24 | 5 | 20X1 | 120s |
| Wk 2 | 24 | 5 | 20X1 | 120s |
| Wk 3 | 24 | 5 | 20X1 | 120s |
| Wk 4 | 24 | 3 | 20X1 | 120s |
| **B1:  Density Seated Dumbbell Curls** | | | | |
| Wk 1 | 10 | 10mins | 10X1 | 0s |
| Wk 2 | 10 | 10mins | 10X1 | 0s |
| Wk 3 | 10 | 10mins | 10X1 | 0s |
| Wk 4 | 10 | 5mins | 10X1 | 0s |
| **B2:  Density Overhead Cable Triceps Extensions** | | | | |
| Wk 1 | 10 | 10mins | 10X1 | 0s |
| Wk 2 | 10 | 10mins | 10X1 | 0s |
| Wk 3 | 10 | 10mins | 10X1 | 0s |
| Wk 4 | 10 | 5mins | 10X1 | 0s |

| Dec | Jan | Feb | Mar | Apr | May |
|---|---|---|---|---|---|
| Phase 1 | Phase 2 | Phase 3 | Phase 4 | Phase 5 | Phase 6 |
| Structural Balance | Accum | Intensification | DUP 1: Strength Density 20 Rep | DUP 2: Waveload Strongman Hypertrophy | DUP 3: Str. Density Strongman Supersets |
| Cond: General Activity | Cond: Genera Activit | Cond: **200m Ev:** Sk:30s, L:35s **120yd Shuttle** Sk:28s L: 33s | Cond: **200m Ev:** Sk:29s, L:33s **120yd Shuttle** Sk:27s L: 33s | Cond: **200m Ev:** Sk:27s, L:32s **120yd Shuttle** Sk:26s L: 33s | Cond: **200m Ev:** Sk:26s, L:31s **120yd Shuttle** Sk:25s L: 32s |

| June | July | Aug | Sept | Oct | Nov |
|---|---|---|---|---|---|
| Phase 7 | Phase 8 | Phase 9 | Phase 10 | Phase 11 | Phase 12 |
| Pre-Summer: Structural Balance | Summer 1 2-a-day | Summer 2 2-a-day | In-Season 1 | In-Season 2 | In-Season 3 |
| Cond: Summer Prep | Cond: Summer SAC Phase 1 | Cond: Summer SAC Phase 2 | Cond: Practice | Cond: Practice | Cond: Practice |

# *EA* Sample One-Year Football S&C Program: **PHASE 9**

# Summer 2-a-Day II

## Duration: 4 Weeks
## Frequency: 8x/week

| Monday | Tuesday | Wednesday | Thursday | Friday | Saturday | Sunday |
|---|---|---|---|---|---|---|
| Summer Phase 2 Day 1: AM | Summer Phase 2 Day 2: AM | Off/recover methods | Summer Phase 2 Day 3: AM | Summer Phase 2 Day 4: AM | Off/recover methods | Off/recover methods |
| Summer Phase 2 Day 1: PM | Summer Phase 2 Day 2: PM | | Summer Phase 2 Day 3: PM | Summer Phase 2 Day 4: PM | | |

## EA Football Phase 9 Summer 2-a-day: Day 1: AM

**Workout:** Lower Body Strength and Power *(Can substitute with lower body French Contrast Program)*

| Week | Reps | Sets | Exercise<br>Tempo | Rest |
|------|------|------|-------|------|
| **A1: Power Clean from the floor** | | | | |
| Wk 1 | 2-4 | 5 | X0X0 | 30s |
| Wk 2 | 2-4 | 5 | X0X0 | 30s |
| Wk 3 | 1-3 | 6 | X0X0 | 30s |
| Wk 4 | 1-2 | 3 | X0X0 | 30s |
| **A2: Depth Jumps** | | | | |
| Wk 1 | 3-4 | 5 | NA | 60s |
| Wk 2 | 3-4 | 5 | NA | 60s |
| Wk 3 | 3-4 | 6 | NA | 60s |
| Wk 4 | 3-4 | 3 | NA | 60s |
| **B1: Back Squat with Chains** | | | | |
| Wk 1 | 3-5 | 5 | 30X1 | 30s |
| Wk 2 | 2-4 | 5 | 30X1 | 30s |
| Wk 3 | 1-3 | 5 | 30X1 | 30s |
| Wk 4 | 1-2 | 3 | 30X1 | 30s |
| **B2: Broad Jump** | | | | |
| Wk 1 | 3-4 | 5 | NA | 30s |
| Wk 2 | 3-4 | 5 | NA | 30s |
| Wk 3 | 3-4 | 5 | NA | 30s |
| Wk 4 | 3-4 | 3 | NA | 30s |
| **B3: Swiss Ball or Kneeling Hamstring Curls** | | | | |
| Wk 1 | 8-10 | 5 | 3010 | 60s |
| Wk 2 | 8-10 | 5 | 3010 | 60s |
| Wk 3 | 8-10 | 5 | 3010 | 60s |
| Wk 4 | 8-10 | 3 | 3010 | 60s |
| **C1: Walking Lunges** | | | | |
| Wk 1 | 12-16 | 3 | 20X0 | 90s |
| Wk 2 | 12-16 | 3 | 20X0 | 90s |
| Wk 3 | 12-16 | 3 | 20X0 | 90s |
| Wk 4 | 12-16 | 1 | 20X0 | 90s |

| Week | Reps | Exercise Sets | Tempo | Rest |
|------|------|------|-------|------|
| **A1: Tire Flips** | | | | |
| Wk 1 | 3-5 | 5 | X0X0 | 30s |
| Wk 2 | 3-4 | 5 | X0X0 | 30s |
| Wk 3 | 2-3 | 6 | X0X0 | 30s |
| Wk 4 | 2-3 | 3 | X0X0 | 30s |
| **A2: 10-15 yd Prowler Acceleration** | | | | |
| Wk 1 | 10-25yds | 5 | NA | 60s |
| Wk 2 | 10-25yds | 5 | NA | 60s |
| Wk 3 | 10-25yds | 5 | NA | 60s |
| Wk 4 | 10-25yds | 3 | NA | 60s |
| **B1: Overhead Med Ball Throws** | | | | |
| Wk 1 | 4-6 | 5 | NA | 30s |
| Wk 2 | 4-6 | 5 | NA | 30s |
| Wk 3 | 4-6 | 5 | NA | 30s |
| Wk 4 | 4-6 | 3 | NA | 30s |
| **B2: Split Jumps** | | | | |
| Wk 1 | 3-4/leg | 5 | NA | 30s |
| Wk 2 | 3-4/leg | 5 | NA | 30s |
| Wk 3 | 3-4/leg | 5 | NA | 30s |
| Wk 4 | 3-4/leg | 3 | NA | 30s |
| **B3: Farmer Carry/HellBarrow** | | | | |
| Wk 1 | 20-40yds | 5 | NA | 60s |
| Wk 2 | 20-40yds | 5 | NA | 60s |
| Wk 3 | 20-40yds | 5 | NA | 60s |
| Wk 4 | 20-40yds | 2 | NA | 60s |
| **C1: Forward down/backward back sled drag** | | | | |
| Wk 1 | 20-40yds | 5 | NA | 90s |
| Wk 2 | 20-40yds | 5 | NA | 90s |
| Wk 3 | 20-40yds | 5 | NA | 90s |
| Wk 4 | 20-40yds | 2 | NA | 60s |

### *EA* Football Phase 9 Summer 2-a-day: Day 2: AM Workout: Upper Body Strength and Power *(Can substitute with upper body French Contrast Program)*

| Week | Reps | Sets | Tempo | Rest |
|------|------|------|-------|------|
| **A1: Flat Barbell Bench Press w/chains** | | | | |
| Wk 1 | 2-4 | 5 | 30X1 | 30s |
| Wk 2 | 2-4 | 5 | 30X1 | 30s |
| Wk 3 | 1-3 | 6 | 30X1 | 30s |
| Wk 4 | 1-2 | 3 | 30X1 | 30s |
| **A2: Jump or clap pushups** | | | | |
| Wk 1 | 3-4 | 5 | NA | 60s |
| Wk 2 | 3-4 | 5 | NA | 60s |
| Wk 3 | 3-4 | 6 | NA | 60s |
| Wk 4 | 3-4 | 3 | NA | 60s |
| **A3: Chin Ups** | | | | |
| Wk 1 | 2-4 | 5 | 30X1 | 30s |
| Wk 2 | 2-4 | 5 | 30X1 | 30s |
| Wk 3 | 1-3 | 6 | 30X1 | 30s |
| Wk 4 | 1-3 | 3 | 30X1 | 30s |
| **A4: Med Ball Slamdowns** | | | | |
| Wk 1 | 6-8 | 5 | NA | 30s |
| Wk 2 | 6-8 | 5 | NA | 30s |
| Wk 3 | 6-8 | 6 | NA | 30s |
| Wk 4 | 6-8 | 3 | NA | 30s |
| **B1: Dips** | | | | |
| Wk 1 | 3-5 | 5 | 3010 | 60s |
| Wk 2 | 3-5 | 5 | 3010 | 60s |
| Wk 3 | 2-4 | 5 | 3010 | 60s |
| Wk 4 | 2-4 | 2 | 3010 | 60s |
| **B2: 1 Arm Dumbbell Rows** | | | | |
| Wk 1 | 3-5 | 5 | 3010 | 60s |
| Wk 2 | 3-5 | 5 | 3010 | 60s |
| Wk 3 | 3-5 | 5 | 3010 | 60s |
| Wk 4 | 3-5 | 2 | 3010 | 60s |
| **C1: Standing Neutral Grip DB Overhead Press** | | | | |
| Wk 1 | 4-6 | 4 | 3010 | 60s |
| Wk 2 | 4-6 | 4 | 3010 | 60s |
| Wk 3 | 4-6 | 4 | 3010 | 60s |
| Wk 4 | 4-6 | 2 | 3010 | 60s |
| **C2: Fat Grip Barbell Curls** | | | | |
| Wk 1 | 4-6 | 4 | 3010 | 60s |
| Wk 2 | 4-6 | 4 | 3010 | 60s |
| Wk 3 | 4-6 | 4 | 3010 | 60s |
| Wk 4 | 4-6 | 2 | 3010 | 60s |

## *EA* Football Phase 9 Summer 2-a-day: Day 2: PM
**Workout:** Upper Body Strongman

| Week | Reps | Sets | Tempo | Rest |
|------|------|------|-------|------|
| **A1: Hand Over Hand Rope Pull** | | | | |
| Wk 1 | 1-2 | 5 | NA | 30s |
| Wk 2 | 1-2 | 5 | NA | 30s |
| Wk 3 | 1-2 | 6 | NA | 30s |
| Wk 4 | 1-2 | 3 | NA | 30s |
| **A2: Overhead Plate or Barbell Carry** | | | | |
| Wk 1 | 20-40yds | 5 | NA | 60s |
| Wk 2 | 20-40yds | 5 | NA | 60s |
| Wk 3 | 20-40yds | 5 | NA | 60s |
| Wk 4 | 20-40yds | 3 | NA | 60s |
| **B1: Hand Over Hand Atlas Stone Slalom Push** | | | | |
| Wk 1 | 20-40yds | 5 | NA | 30s |
| Wk 2 | 20-40yds | 5 | NA | 30s |
| Wk 3 | 20-40yds | 5 | NA | 30s |
| Wk 4 | 20-40yds | 3 | NA | 30s |
| **B2: Sledgehammer Sand or Tire Hits** | | | | |
| Wk 1 | 20 | 5 | NA | 60s |
| Wk 2 | 20 | 5 | NA | 60s |
| Wk 3 | 20 | 5 | NA | 60s |
| Wk 4 | 20 | 3 | NA | 60s |
| **C: Burpees for Height** | | | | |
| Wk 1 | 15 | 5 | NA | 60s |
| Wk 2 | 15 | 5 | NA | 60s |
| Wk 3 | 15 | 5 | NA | 60s |
| Wk 4 | 15 | 2 | NA | 60s |

**Workout:** Lower Body Strength and Power *(Can substitute with lower body French Contrast Program)*

| Week | Reps | Sets | Exercise Tempo | Rest |
|------|------|------|-------|------|
| **A1: High Pull to Deadlift (Sets 1-3HP/Sets4-6DL)** | | | | |
| Wk 1 | 3-5 | 6 | X0X0 | 30s |
| Wk 2 | 2-4 | 6 | X0X0 | 30s |
| Wk 3 | 1-3 | 6 | X0X0 | 30s |
| Wk 4 | 1-2 | 3 | X0X0 | 30s |
| **A2: Depth Jumps** | | | | |
| Wk 1 | 3-4 | 6 | NA | 60s |
| Wk 2 | 3-4 | 6 | NA | 60s |
| Wk 3 | 3-4 | 6 | NA | 60s |
| Wk 4 | 3-4 | 3 | NA | 60s |
| **B1: Front Squat** | | | | |
| Wk 1 | 3-5 | 5 | 30X1 | 30s |
| Wk 2 | 3-4 | 5 | 30X1 | 30s |
| Wk 3 | 2-4 | 5 | 30X1 | 30s |
| Wk 4 | 2-3 | 3 | 30X1 | 30s |
| **B2: 5-10-5** | | | | |
| Wk 1 | 1 | 5 | NA | 30s |
| Wk 2 | 1 | 5 | NA | 30s |
| Wk 3 | 1 | 5 | NA | 30s |
| Wk 4 | 1 | 3 | NA | 30s |
| **C1: Glute Ham Raise** | | | | |
| Wk 1 | 6-8 | 5 | 3010 | 60s |
| Wk 2 | 5-7 | 5 | 3010 | 60s |
| Wk 3 | 4-6 | 5 | 3010 | 60s |
| Wk 4 | 4-6 | 2 | 3010 | 60s |
| **C2: Alternating Leg Step Forward Lunges** | | | | |
| Wk 1 | 12-16 | 3 | 20X0 | 90s |
| Wk 2 | 12-16 | 3 | 20X0 | 90s |
| Wk 3 | 12-16 | 3 | 20X0 | 90s |
| Wk 4 | 12-16 | 2 | 20X0 | 90s |

## *EA* Football Phase 9 Summer 2-a-day: Day 3: PM
### Workout: Density Legs (Strength Emphasis)

| Week | Reps | Sets | Exercise Tempo | Rest |
|------|------|------|-------|------|
| **A: Barbell Back Squat (Teams of 3)** | | | | |
| Wk 1 | 3 | 20min | 30X1 | N |
| Wk 2 | 3 | 20mins | 30X1 | N |
| Wk 3 | 3 | 20mins | 30X1 | N |
| Wk 4 | 3 | 10mins | 30X1 | N |
| **B: Prowler Push** | | | | |
| Wk 1 | 20-30yds | 10 | NA | 60s |
| Wk 2 | 20-30yds | 10 | NA | 60s |
| Wk 3 | 20-30yds | 10 | NA | 60s |
| Wk 4 | 20-30yds | 5 | NA | 60s |

## *EA* Football Phase 9 Summer 2-a-day: Day 4: AM
Workout: Upper Body Strength and Power *(Can substitute with upper body French Contrast Program)*

|          |       |      | Exercise |      |
|----------|-------|------|----------|------|
| Week     | Reps  | Sets | Tempo    | Rest |
| **A1:  Push Press or Jerk** | | | | |
| Wk 1     | 3-5   | 5    | 10X1     | 30s  |
| Wk 2     | 3-4   | 5    | 10X1     | 30s  |
| Wk 3     | 2-3   | 6    | 10X1     | 30s  |
| Wk 4     | 2-3   | 3    | 10X1     | 30s  |
| **B1:  Incline DB Bench Press** | | | | |
| Wk 1     | 3-5   | 5    | 30X1     | 30s  |
| Wk 2     | 3-4   | 5    | 30X1     | 30s  |
| Wk 3     | 2-4   | 6    | 30X1     | 30s  |
| Wk 4     | 1-3   | 3    | 30X1     | 30s  |
| **B2: Chest Pass Med Ball Throws** | | | | |
| Wk 1     | 3-4   | 5    | NA       | 60s  |
| Wk 2     | 3-4   | 5    | NA       | 60s  |
| Wk 3     | 3-4   | 6    | NA       | 60s  |
| Wk 4     | 3-4   | 3    | NA       | 60s  |
| **B3:  Pull-ups** | | | | |
| Wk 1     | 3-5   | 5    | 30X1     | 30s  |
| Wk 2     | 3-4   | 5    | 30X1     | 30s  |
| Wk 3     | 2-4   | 6    | 30X1     | 30s  |
| Wk 4     | 1-3   | 3    | 30X1     | 30s  |
| **B4: Power Sled Pull** | | | | |
| Wk 1     | 6-8   | 5    | NA       | 30s  |
| Wk 2     | 6-8   | 5    | NA       | 30s  |
| Wk 3     | 6-8   | 6    | NA       | 30s  |
| Wk 4     | 6-8   | 3    | NA       | 30s  |
| **C1: Dips** | | | | |
| Wk 1     | 4-6   | 5    | 3010     | 60s  |
| Wk 2     | 3-5   | 5    | 3010     | 60s  |
| Wk 3     | 3-5   | 5    | 3010     | 60s  |
| Wk 4     | 3-5   | 3    | 3010     | 60s  |
| **C2: Seated Cable Rows** | | | | |
| Wk 1     | 4-6   | 5    | 3010     | 60s  |
| Wk 2     | 4-6   | 5    | 3010     | 60s  |
| Wk 3     | 4-6   | 5    | 3010     | 60s  |
| Wk 4     | 4-6   | 3    | 3010     | 60s  |

## *EA* Football Phase 9 Summer 2-a-day: Day 4: PM

**Workout:** Upper Body Hypertrophy

| Week | Reps | Sets | Tempo | Rest |
|------|------|------|-------|------|
| **A1: Dips** | | | | |
| Wk 1 | 6-8 | 5 | 30X1 | 60s |
| Wk 2 | 6-8 | 5 | 30X1 | 60s |
| Wk 3 | 6-7 | 5 | 30X1 | 60s |
| Wk 4 | 6-7 | 3 | 30X1 | 60s |
| **A2: Neutral Grip Chin Ups** | | | | |
| Wk 1 | 6-8 | 5 | 30X1 | 60s |
| Wk 2 | 6-8 | 5 | 30X1 | 60s |
| Wk 3 | 6-7 | 5 | 30X1 | 60s |
| Wk 4 | 6-7 | 3 | 30X1 | 60s |
| **B1: Flat DB Bench Press** | | | | |
| Wk 1 | 6-8 | 5 | 30X1 | 60s |
| Wk 2 | 6-8 | 5 | 30X1 | 60s |
| Wk 3 | 6-7 | 5 | 30X1 | 60s |
| Wk 4 | 6-7 | 3 | 30X1 | 60s |
| **B2: Inverted Ring Rows** | | | | |
| Wk 1 | 6-8 | 5 | 30X1 | 60s |
| Wk 2 | 6-8 | 5 | 30X1 | 60s |
| Wk 3 | 6-7 | 5 | 30X1 | 60s |
| Wk 4 | 6-7 | 3 | 30X1 | 60s |
| **C1: Seated Hammer Curls** | | | | |
| Wk 1 | 6 | 5 | 2010 | 20s |
| Wk 2 | 6 | 5 | 2010 | 20s |
| Wk 3 | 6 | 6 | 2010 | 20s |
| Wk 4 | 6 | 3 | 2010 | 20s |
| **C2: Standing DB Curls** | | | | |
| Wk 1 | 12 | 5 | 2010 | 60s |
| Wk 2 | 12 | 5 | 2010 | 60s |
| Wk 3 | 12 | 5 | 2010 | 60s |
| Wk 4 | 12 | 3 | 2010 | 60s |
| **C3: Overhead DB Triceps Extensions** | | | | |
| Wk 1 | 6 | 5 | 2010 | 20s |
| Wk 2 | 6 | 5 | 2010 | 20s |
| Wk 3 | 6 | 6 | 2010 | 20s |
| Wk 4 | 6 | 3 | 2010 | 20s |
| **C4: Close Grip (Triceps Emphasis) Pushups** | | | | |
| Wk 1 | 12 | 5 | 2010 | 60s |
| Wk 2 | 12 | 5 | 2010 | 60s |
| Wk 3 | 12 | 5 | 2010 | 60s |
| Wk 4 | 12 | 3 | 2010 | 60s |

| Dec | Jan | Feb | Mar | Apr | May |
|---|---|---|---|---|---|
| Phase 1 | Phase 2 | Phase 3 | Phase 4 | Phase 5 | Phase 6 |
| Structural Balance | Accum | Intensification | DUP 1: Strength Density 20 Rep | DUP 2: Waveload Strongman Hypertrophy | DUP 3: Str. Density Strongman Supersets |
| Cond: General Activity | Cond: Genera Activit | Cond: **200m Ev:** Sk:30s, L:35s **120yd Shuttle** Sk:28s L: 33s | Cond: **200m Ev:** Sk:29s, L:33s **120yd Shuttle** Sk:27s L: 33s | Cond: **200m Ev:** Sk:27s, L:32s **120yd Shuttle** Sk:26s L: 33s | Cond: **200m Ev:** Sk:26s, L:31s **120yd Shuttle** Sk:25s L: 32s |

| June | July | Aug | Sept | Oct | Nov |
|---|---|---|---|---|---|
| Phase 7 | Phase 8 | Phase 9 | Phase 10 | Phase 11 | Phase 12 |
| Pre-Summer: Structural Balance | Summer 1 2-a-day | Summer 2 2-a-day | In-Season 1 | In-Season 2 | In-Season 3 |
| Cond: Summer Prep | Cond: Summer SAC Phase 1 | Cond: Summer SAC Phase 2 | Cond: Practice | Cond: Practice | Cond: Practice |

# *EA* Sample One-Year Football S&C Program: **PHASE 10**

## In-Season I

## **Duration:** 4 Weeks
## **Frequency:** 2x/week

| Monday | Tuesday | Wednesday | Thursday | Friday | Saturday | Sunday |
|---|---|---|---|---|---|---|
| In-Season Phase 1 Day 1: Hypert | Off/recover methods | In-Season Phase 1 Day 2: Strength power | Off/recover methods | GAME NIGHT | Off/recover methods | Off/recover methods |

## *EA* Football Phase 10: In-Season 1:Day 1: Hypertrophy

| Week | Reps | Exercise Sets | Tempo | Rest |
|------|------|------|-------|------|
| **A1:  Front Squat** | | | | |
| Wk 1 | 5-6 | 3 | 41X1 | 60s |
| Wk 2 | 5-6 | 3 | 41X1 | 60s |
| Wk 3 | 4-6 | 3 | 41X1 | 60s |
| Wk 4 | 4-6 | 2 | 41X1 | 60s |
| **A2: Flat DB Bench Press** | | | | |
| Wk 1 | 8-10 | 3 | 3010 | 60s |
| Wk 2 | 8-10 | 3 | 3010 | 60s |
| Wk 3 | 7-9 | 3 | 3010 | 60s |
| Wk 4 | 7-9 | 2 | 3010 | 60s |
| **B1:  Glute Ham Raise** | | | | |
| Wk 1 | 6-8 | 3 | 3010 | 60s |
| Wk 2 | 6-8 | 3 | 3010 | 60s |
| Wk 3 | 5-7 | 3 | 3010 | 60s |
| Wk 4 | 5-7 | 2 | 3010 | 60s |
| **B2: Inverted Ring Rows** | | | | |
| Wk 1 | 8-10 | 3 | 3010 | 60s |
| Wk 2 | 8-10 | 3 | 3010 | 60s |
| Wk 3 | 7-9 | 3 | 3010 | 60s |
| Wk 4 | 7-9 | 2 | 3010 | 60s |
| **C: Y,T,L** | | | | |
| Wk 1 | 10,10,10 | 3 | 2010 | 60s |
| Wk 2 | 10,10,10 | 3 | 2010 | 60s |
| Wk 3 | 10,10,10 | 3 | 2010 | 60s |
| Wk 4 | 10,10,10 | 2 | 2010 | 60s |

## *EA* Football Phase 10: In-Season 1:Day 2: Strength and Power

| Week | Reps | Sets | Exercise Tempo | Rest |
|------|------|------|--------|------|
| **A1: Power Clean from hang above knee** | | | | |
| Wk 1 | 3-5 | 3 | X0X0 | 30s |
| Wk 2 | 3-4 | 3 | X0X0 | 30s |
| Wk 3 | 2-3 | 3 | X0X0 | 30s |
| Wk 4 | 2-3 | 2 | X0X0 | 30s |
| **A2: Vertical Jump** | | | | |
| Wk 1 | 3 | 3 | | 120s |
| Wk 2 | 3 | 3 | | 120s |
| Wk 3 | 3 | 3 | | 120s |
| Wk 4 | 3 | 2 | | 120s |
| **B1: Back Squat** | | | | |
| Wk 1 | 3-5 | 3 | 31X1 | 60s |
| Wk 2 | 3-5 | 3 | 31X1 | 60s |
| Wk 3 | 3-5 | 3 | 31X1 | 60s |
| Wk 4 | 3-5 | 2 | 31X1 | 60s |
| **B2: Dips** | | | | |
| Wk 1 | 3-5 | 3 | 30X1 | 60s |
| Wk 2 | 3-5 | 3 | 30X1 | 60s |
| Wk 3 | 3-5 | 3 | 30X1 | 60s |
| Wk 4 | 3-5 | 2 | 30X1 | 60s |
| **C1: Hamstring Curl Variation** | | | | |
| Wk 1 | 5-7 | 3 | 20X0 | 60s |
| Wk 2 | 4-6 | 3 | 20X0 | 60s |
| Wk 3 | 3-5 | 3 | 20X0 | 60s |
| Wk 4 | 3-5 | 2 | 20X0 | 60s |
| **C2: Chin Ups** | | | | |
| Wk 1 | 3-5 | 3 | 30X1 | 60s |
| Wk 2 | 3-5 | 3 | 30X1 | 60s |
| Wk 3 | 3-5 | 3 | 30X1 | 60s |
| Wk 4 | 3-5 | 2 | 30X1 | 60s |

| Dec | Jan | Feb | Mar | Apr | May |
|---|---|---|---|---|---|
| Phase 1 | Phase 2 | Phase 3 | Phase 4 | Phase 5 | Phase 6 |
| Structural Balance | Accum | Intensification | DUP 1: Strength Density 20 Rep | DUP 2: Waveload Strongman Hypertrophy | DUP 3: Str. Density Strongman Supersets |
| Cond: General Activity | Cond: Genera Activit | Cond: **200m Ev:** Sk:30s, L:35s **120yd Shuttle** Sk:28s L: 33s | Cond: **200m Ev:** Sk:29s, L:33s **120yd Shuttle** Sk:27s L: 33s | Cond: **200m Ev:** Sk:27s, L:32s **120yd Shuttle** Sk:26s L: 33s | Cond: **200m Ev:** Sk:26s, L:31s **120yd Shuttle** Sk:25s L: 32s |

| June | July | Aug | Sept | Oct | Nov |
|---|---|---|---|---|---|
| Phase 7 | Phase 8 | Phase 9 | Phase 10 | Phase 11 | Phase 12 |
| Pre-Summer: Structural Balance | Summer 1 2-a-day | Summer 2 2-a-day | In-Season 1 | In-Season 2 | In-Season 3 |
| Cond: Summer Prep | Cond: Summer SAC Phase 1 | Cond: Summer SAC Phase 2 | Cond: Practice | Cond: Practice | Cond: Practice |

# *EA* Sample One-Year Football S&C Program: **PHASE 11**

## In-Season II

### Duration: 4 Weeks
### Frequency: 2x/week

| Monday | Tuesday | Wednesday | Thursday | Friday | Saturday | Sunday |
|---|---|---|---|---|---|---|
| In-Season Phase 1 Day 1: Hypert | Off/recover methods | In-Season Phase 1 Day 2: Strength power | Off/recover methods | *GAME NIGHT* | Off/recover methods | Off/recover methods |

## _EA_ Football Phase 11: In-Season Phase 2: Day 1:
Hypertrophy

| Week | Reps | Exercise Sets | Tempo | Rest |
|------|------|------|-------|------|
| | **A1: Rack Pull** | | | |
| Wk 1 | 8-10 | 3 | 30X1 | 60s |
| Wk 2 | 8-10 | 3 | 30X1 | 60s |
| Wk 3 | 7-9 | 3 | 30X1 | 60s |
| Wk 4 | 6-8 | 2 | 30X1 | 60s |
| | **A2: Dips** | | | |
| Wk 1 | 8-10 | 3 | 3011 | 60s |
| Wk 2 | 8-10 | 3 | 3011 | 60s |
| Wk 3 | 7-9 | 3 | 3011 | 60s |
| Wk 4 | 7-9 | 2 | 3011 | 60s |
| | **B1: Barbell Back Squat** | | | |
| Wk 1 | 8-10 | 3 | 30X1 | 60s |
| Wk 2 | 8-10 | 3 | 30X1 | 60s |
| Wk 3 | 7-9 | 3 | 30X1 | 60s |
| Wk 4 | 6-8 | 2 | 30X1 | 60s |
| | **B2: Chin Ups** | | | |
| Wk 1 | 8-10 | 3 | 3010 | 60s |
| Wk 2 | 8-10 | 3 | 3010 | 60s |
| Wk 3 | 7-9 | 3 | 3010 | 60s |
| Wk 4 | 7-9 | 2 | 3010 | 60s |
| | **C: Y,T,L** | | | |
| Wk 1 | 10,10,10 | 3 | 2010 | 60s |
| Wk 2 | 10,10,10 | 3 | 2010 | 60s |
| Wk 3 | 10,10,10 | 3 | 2010 | 60s |
| Wk 4 | 10,10,10 | 2 | 2010 | 60s |

## *EA* Football Phase 11: In-Season Phase 2: Day 2: Strength and Power

| Week | Reps | Sets | Exercise Tempo | Rest |
|------|------|------|----------------|------|
| **A1: Power Clean from hang below knee** | | | | |
| Wk 1 | 3-5 | 3 | X0X0 | 30s |
| Wk 2 | 3-4 | 3 | X0X0 | 30s |
| Wk 3 | 2-3 | 3 | X0X0 | 30s |
| Wk 4 | 2-3 | 2 | X0X0 | 30s |
| **A2: Vertical Jump** | | | | |
| Wk 1 | 3 | 3 | | 120s |
| Wk 2 | 3 | 3 | | 120s |
| Wk 3 | 3 | 3 | | 120s |
| Wk 4 | 3 | 2 | | 120s |
| **B1: Front Squat** | | | | |
| Wk 1 | 3-5 | 3 | 31X1 | 60s |
| Wk 2 | 3-5 | 3 | 31X1 | 60s |
| Wk 3 | 3-4 | 3 | 31X1 | 60s |
| Wk 4 | 2-3 | 2 | 31X1 | 60s |
| **B2: Flat Barbell Bench Press** | | | | |
| Wk 1 | 3-5 | 3 | 30X1 | 60s |
| Wk 2 | 3-5 | 3 | 30X1 | 60s |
| Wk 3 | 3-4 | 3 | 30X1 | 60s |
| Wk 4 | 2-3 | 2 | 30X1 | 60s |
| **C1: Alternating Leg Step Forward Lunges** | | | | |
| Wk 1 | 4-6/leg | 3 | 20X0 | 60s |
| Wk 2 | 4-6/leg | 3 | 20X0 | 60s |
| Wk 3 | 3-5/leg | 3 | 20X0 | 60s |
| Wk 4 | 3-5/leg | 2 | 20X0 | 60s |
| **C2: Pull-Up** | | | | |
| Wk 1 | 3-5 | 3 | 30X1 | 60s |
| Wk 2 | 3-5 | 3 | 30X1 | 60s |
| Wk 3 | 3-4 | 3 | 30X1 | 60s |
| Wk 4 | 2-3 | 2 | 30X1 | 60s |

| Dec | Jan | Feb | Mar | Apr | May |
|---|---|---|---|---|---|
| Phase 1 | Phase 2 | Phase 3 | Phase 4 | Phase 5 | Phase 6 |
| Structural Balance | Accum | Intensification | DUP 1: Strength Density 20 Rep | DUP 2: Waveload Strongman Hypertrophy | DUP 3: Str. Density Strongman Supersets |
| Cond: General Activity | Cond: Genera Activit | Cond: **200m Ev:** Sk:30s, L:35s **120yd Shuttle** Sk:28s L: 33s | Cond: **200m Ev:** Sk:29s, L:33s **120yd Shuttle** Sk:27s L: 33s | Cond: **200m Ev:** Sk:27s, L:32s **120yd Shuttle** Sk:26s L: 33s | Cond: **200m Ev:** Sk:26s, L:31s **120yd Shuttle** Sk:25s L: 32s |

| June | July | Aug | Sept | Oct | Nov |
|---|---|---|---|---|---|
| Phase 7 | Phase 8 | Phase 9 | Phase 10 | Phase 11 | Phase 12 |
| Pre-Summer: Structural Balance | Summer 1 2-a-day | Summer 2 2-a-day | In-Season 1 | In-Season 2 | In-Season 3 |
| Cond: Summer Prep | Cond: Summer SAC Phase 1 | Cond: Summer SAC Phase 2 | Cond: Practice | Cond: Practice | Cond: Practice |

# *EA* Sample One-Year Football S&C Program: **PHASE 12**

## In-Season III

## **Duration:** 4 Weeks
## **Frequency:** 2x/week

| Monday | Tuesday | Wednesday | Thursday | Friday | Saturday | Sunday |
|---|---|---|---|---|---|---|
| In-Season Phase 1 Day 1: Hypert | Off/recover methods | In-Season Phase 1 Day 2: Strength power | Off/recover methods | *GAME NIGHT* | Off/recover methods | Off/recover methods |

# _EA_ Football Phase 12: In-Season Phase 3: Day 1: Hypertrophy

| Week | Reps | Exercise<br>Sets | Tempo | Rest |
|------|------|------|-------|------|
| **A1:  Deadlift** | | | | |
| Wk 1 | 8-10 | 3 | 1010 | 60s |
| Wk 2 | 7-9 | 3 | 1010 | 60s |
| Wk 3 | 6-8 | 3 | 1010 | 60s |
| Wk 4 | 5-7 | 2 | 1010 | 60s |
| **A2: Incline DB Bench Pres** | | | | |
| Wk 1 | 8-10 | 3 | 30X0 | 60s |
| Wk 2 | 7-9 | 3 | 30X0 | 60s |
| Wk 3 | 6-8 | 3 | 30X0 | 60s |
| Wk 4 | 6-8 | 2 | 30X0 | 60s |
| **B1:  Alternating Leg Drop Lunges** | | | | |
| Wk 1 | 8-10/leg | 3 | 20X0 | 60s |
| Wk 2 | 7-9/leg | 3 | 20X0 | 60s |
| Wk 3 | 6-8/leg | 3 | 20X0 | 60s |
| Wk 4 | 6-8/leg | 2 | 20X0 | 60s |
| **B2: Chin Ups** | | | | |
| Wk 1 | 8-10 | 3 | 3010 | 60s |
| Wk 2 | 7-9 | 3 | 3010 | 60s |
| Wk 3 | 6-8 | 3 | 3010 | 60s |
| Wk 4 | 6-8 | 2 | 3010 | 60s |
| **C: Y,T,L** | | | | |
| Wk 1 | 10,10,10 | 3 | 2010 | 60s |
| Wk 2 | 10,10,10 | 3 | 2010 | 60s |
| Wk 3 | 10,10,10 | 3 | 2010 | 60s |
| Wk 4 | 10,10,10 | 2 | 2010 | 60s |

## *EA* Football Phase 12: In-Season Phase 3: Day 2:
Strength and Power

| Week | Reps | Exercise Sets | Tempo | Rest |
|------|------|------|-------|------|
| | | **A1: Power Clean from floor** | | |
| Wk 1 | 3-5 | 3 | X0X0 | 30s |
| Wk 2 | 3-4 | 3 | X0X0 | 30s |
| Wk 3 | 2-3 | 3 | X0X0 | 30s |
| Wk 4 | 2-3 | 2 | X0X0 | 30s |
| | | **A2: Vertical Jump** | | |
| Wk 1 | 3 | 3 | | 120s |
| Wk 2 | 3 | 3 | | 120s |
| Wk 3 | 3 | 3 | | 120s |
| Wk 4 | 3 | 2 | | 120s |
| | | **B1: Back Squat** | | |
| Wk 1 | 3-5 | 3 | 31X1 | 60s |
| Wk 2 | 3-5 | 3 | 31X1 | 60s |
| Wk 3 | 3-4 | 3 | 31X1 | 60s |
| Wk 4 | 2-3 | 2 | 31X1 | 60s |
| | | **B2: Flat Barbell Bench Press** | | |
| Wk 1 | 3-5 | 3 | 30X1 | 60s |
| Wk 2 | 3-5 | 3 | 30X1 | 60s |
| Wk 3 | 3-4 | 3 | 30X1 | 60s |
| Wk 4 | 2-3 | 2 | 30X1 | 60s |
| | | **C1: Glute Ham Raise** | | |
| Wk 1 | 4-6 | 3 | 3010 | 60s |
| Wk 2 | 4-6 | 3 | 3010 | 60s |
| Wk 3 | 3-5 | 3 | 3010 | 60s |
| Wk 4 | 3-5 | 2 | 3010 | 60s |
| | | **C2: Close Neutral Grip Chin Ups** | | |
| Wk 1 | 3-5 | 3 | 2010 | 60s |
| Wk 2 | 3-5 | 3 | 2010 | 60s |
| Wk 3 | 3-4 | 3 | 2010 | 60s |
| Wk 4 | 2-3 | 2 | 2010 | 60s |

# 8 WEEK
# FOOTBALL
## *SPEED, AGILITY, and*
## *CONDITIONING PROGRAM*

# SPEED, AGILITY, AND CONDITIONING OVERVIEW

*"To finish first, preparation cannot come second"*

Athletes are built in the off-season. The ability to dedicate oneself to an off-season strength and conditioning program is half the battle for many athletes. The on-field experience is the fun part.

To prepare optimally/adequately, athletes should not decide two weeks before the beginning of tryouts that they are going to get in shape. This is a strategy for overuse, problematic overload, and acute or chronic injury.

## *"Fatigue makes cowards of all men".*

There is a saying in the sports world *"fatigue makes cowards of all men".* Changing an athlete's mindset when it comes to the "conditioning" component can be a valuable tool to both athletes and coaches. When athletes begin to view conditioning as a privilege or opportunity to get better, and have their teammates backs, the results can be significant.

An athlete's belief and trust in his/her teammates can be built, along with speed, toughness, and conditioning, over time. The body needs time to adapt, recover, and supercompensate. With that said, high levels of metabolic conditioning are not created two weeks prior to the start of tryouts. Instead, they are built over weeks or months of structured workouts, prior to tryouts.

Approaching metabolic conditioning blindly, can lead to issues including lack of adherence, regression rather than progression, and an invite to the cumulative injury cycle, which plagues many athletes.

# Building Trust

## Learning to Run Through Walls and Have Your Teammates Backs:

During the fall and early winter months, we see it on any given Friday night, Saturday afternoon, or Sunday. Successful football teams in which the players have "bought in". These players trust in their coaches and coaching staff. These players have each other's backs and will run through walls for each other and their coaches. As the New England Patriots so eloquently put it "Do your job". This same team building culture can also be seen in the military. Officers and enlisted soldiers working for each other, having each other's backs and "doing their jobs".

One thread each of these organizational types have in common is how this "running through walls, working for each other, and having your teammates back's" culture is built. In the military it is called boot camp. In law-enforcement it is called an academy. In football it is called off-season and pre-season.


### Using Speed, Agility, and Conditioning to teach athletes to run through walls for each other and have each other's backs.

The following method of SAC training has three purposes:

1. Get athletes working for each other

213

2. Help expose leadership and *"divaship"*

3. Teach athletes to push through **self-imposed** plateaus and work as hard as they can toward common team goal.

How this is done:

1. **Rule 1:** Athletes must push as hard as they can per sprint/drill. *"You cannot fake effort!"*. Body language and the watch do not lie.

2. **Rule 2:** All athletes must sprint through the line.

3. **Rule 3**: All instructions must be followed perfectly.

4. **Rule 4:** If athletes are not putting forth best/full effort they can sit out any time they want after mandatory sprints/drill done.

## Understanding the Template

**Sample Template:**

| Exercise | Sets | Reps | Intensity | Tempo | Rest Interval |
|----------|------|------|-----------|-------|---------------|
| Timed 40's | 1 2 3 4 | 40yds < 6s 40yds < 6s 40yds <6s 40yds < 6s | NA | NA | 50s |

Each template contains 6 columns: exercise, sets, reps, intensity, tempo, and rest interval. Below each column title is the numeric prescription for that variable. Below is a breakdown of how to read each variable.

1. **Exercise:** This column is self-explanatory. The prescribed exercise is found in this column. Some templates have a small description of the exercise or slight changes in the performance of the exercise.

2. **Sets:** Each number in the column represents a set. The last number is total number of sets to be performed for the prescribed exercise. The repetition count which is parallel to the set # describes how many reps are done in that particular set.

3. **Rest interval:** This is the rest time between sets (or reps for some exercises). At the completion of a set, the clock starts. Once the allotted time has elapsed, the next set begins.

**Warm-Up:** This section of the template is designed to increase the body's core temperature, create structural alignment of the load bearing joints, and increase activation of the central nervous system. Each of these exercises is designed in sequence from least to greatest activation of the CNS.

**Warm-up Exercise Descriptions**

**Active Warm Up:** This consists of 20 yards intervals of the following exercises:

- Jog

- High Knees

- Butt Kickers

- Carioca

- Back Pedal

- Low Skips

- Power Skips

- Skater Hops

- Side Shuffle

- Hip Flexor Stretch to lunge

- Hip Extensor Stretch to step

**Postural Correction Exercises:**

Before you begin, try this exercise. Close your eyes and slowly march in place for 5 seconds. After you stop marching, keep your eyes closed and notice where your weight distribution is. Try to feel if you have more weight on one foot vs. the other foot, or more weight on the toes vs. heels of both feet. If your weight is not evenly distributed, you may have postural imbalances which can lead to improper movement or dysfunction. It is important to try to modify/correct these imbalances before you begin a workout. The following exercises are just an example of some exercises which can help rebalance an athlete's weight distribution. Upon completion of these exercises (when done correctly), march in place with your eyes closed and see if you can notice a difference in weight distribution.

- **Hand/Arm Circles:** Stand with feet parallel about 1 fist apart. Standing upright with arms at your sides and retract (pull) your shoulder blades as far back as possible. While pulling back, pull shoulder blades down without leaning/arching backward. Maintaining shoulder position, begin raising your arms out to your sides (abduct) with your palms facing downward, with your distal 2 knuckles of each finger closed and thumb pointing forward. Begin rotating your arms in small counterclockwise circles without allowing your shoulder

217

to elevate or protract. Once you have completed the prescribed number of repetitions, rotate arms in a clockwise direction for the prescribed number of reps. You should feel these between and just below the shoulder blades.

- **Horizontal Elbow Ab/Adductions:** Stand with feet parallel about 1 fist apart. With palms facing away, bring both hands up to your temples and place your second knuckle of each finger at your temples. Maintaining contact with the temples, touch both elbows together in front of your face, with the triceps parallel to the floor. Maintaining parallel to the floor with the upper arms, slowly depress your shoulder blades and pull your elbows apart as far as possible until they are completely at your sides, with your shoulder blades pinched together. Then bring elbows back to touching and repeat for the prescribed number of repetitions.

- **Postural Shoulder Shrugs:** Stand with feet parallel about 1 fist wide. Keeping arms at your sides, begin by pulling (retracting) your shoulder blades as far as you can. From here, pull them down, pinching the musculature about the shoulder blades. Rotate your shoulders to the front and elevate them as far as you can. From here retract and repeat the sequence for the prescribed number of repetitions.

- **Standing Overhead Reach and Retract:** Stand with feet parallel about 1 fits apart. Interlock fingers in front of you and rotate palms outward, with interlocked fingers and palms facing outward, raise your arms up over your head until they are directly overhead (not behind you). Maintaining straight arms, pull your shoulder blades down and back, being careful not to lean back or arch too much. Hold this position for the prescribed time.

## Hip Mobility Circuit:

- **Fire Hydrants:** Position yourself on your hands and knees. With 90 degree bend in the knee, raise your leg out to your side until the upper thigh is parallel to the floor. From this position, begin extending the leg backward until the leg/hip is fully extended and the upper thigh is parallel to the floor. Return to start and repeat for the prescribed repetitions prior to working the other leg.

- **Side Lying Hip Raises Vertical:** Lay on your side with straight legs stacked on top of each other. Flex at the hips until you have about a 130-160degree angle at the hips.

Begin by elevating the foot of the top leg about 12-24 inches, maintaining a fully extended leg. Lower slowly and perform for the prescribed amount of repetitions. **Side Lying Hip Raises Horizontal:** Upon completion of vertical raises you will immediately perform horizontal raises on the same leg. Begin with the top foot on the ground about 24 inches in front of the bottom foot. Elevate foot until and extend hip until the top foot is 24 inches directly above the bottom foot, and slowly lower back to the start position.

- **Wall Facing Squats:** Begin by facing a wall with feet slightly wider than normal squat stance. Pointing toes about 15-30 degrees outward, position feet against the wall so your toes touch the wall. Place your hands on top of your head. Begin to squat down allowing your knees to come in contact with the wall. Squat as low as you can without falling over and repeat for the prescribed number of repetitions. Your goal should be to squat with your hips below your knees as this creates ideal hip mobility.

**Postural Bear Crawl:** Position yourself on your hands and knees, with your knees directly below your hips and your hands directly below your shoulders. From this position, arch your back as much as you can. While maintaining this arch, raise your knees 1-2 inches off the ground. Keeping your knees below your hips and back arched, begin crawling on your hands and feet for the prescribed distance.

**Squat/Lunge/Jump Squat Series:** Perform the prescribed number of bodyweight squats, immediately followed by step forward lunges, then jump squats for the prescribed number of reps.

## Speed, Agility, Jumping, and Metabolic Conditioning Exercise Descriptions

**Having Your Teammates Back Sprints:** Named after the researcher who performed studies on subjects to determine the effectiveness of different work to rest intervals. He found that a 20 second rest followed by 10 second recovery for 4 minutes was highly effective for development of metabolic condition. Here the athlete will perform the prescribed exercise for 20 seconds, rest 10 and repeat for 4 minutes. Be sure to follow the guidelines in the exercise box on the actual template.

- 5yd line ⮕ goal line ⮕ 10yd line change of direction acceleration sprints
- 10yds line ⮕ goal line ⮕ 20 yd line change of direction acceleration sprints

221

- Timed or team 30yd sprints
- Timed or team 40 yd sprints
- Timed or team 60yd sprints
- Timed or team 80yds sprints
- Timed or Team 200 yd sprints
- Team 5 yard wide/5 yard deep slaloms
- Hills

**Multi-Directional Sprints:** As sport consists of rapid changes of direction, so should an athlete's training. Without rapid change of direction training, an athlete may lack in development of agility and acceleration, which may not only compromise on-field performance, but also increase the risk of injury. Most athletic knee injuries occur during a deceleration and change of direction in which the mechanics are altered. This alteration may be due to improper posture, weakness, neuromuscular deficiency, technical deficiency, lack of training/practice, or fatigue.

**Autoregulatory Sprints:** Your body regulates your performance. Your performance in turn regulates how many sprints you do.

**Timed Sprints:** The distance is given. The goal time is given. The number of sprints you need to complete is given, and the rest interval between sprints is given. Not much more need to be said.

**Jumping/Reactive Exercises:** Read the description in the neuromuscular warm up section for the correct technique. Now they are done with speed for greater distances with less time for recovery.

- Single Leg Broad Jump
- Pushup position to full hip extension broad/vertical jump
- Skater hops (stick the landing for 2s)
- 30 yd power skip
- Change of direction single leg broad jump

# 8 Week Football Speed, Agility, and Conditioning Program

## Guidelines:

1. SAC Trained 3X/Week Weights 4-8X/Week (*this is only the metabolic program).
2. The program is broken into 4-week accumulation and 1 week recovery/low volume, 2 week intensification/accumulation 1 week recovery/low volume.
3. Goal of this program is to teach the athletes to put their best effort forward while learning to work for each other and hold each other accountable.

### Rules

1. **Rule 1:** "If you are not getting better, you're getting worse". (Pat Riley)

2. **Rule 2:** If you are sprinting, do so with all-out effort. You cannot fake body language.
3. **Rule 3:** ALWAYS SPRINT THROUGH THE LINE.
4. **Rule 4:** Coaches determine at what point athletes can sit out if they are not putting forth full effort.
5. **Rule 5:** If rule 1 and/or rule 2 are broken, that sprint does not count. Only quality sprints count.

# Week 1

## *EA* Football *SAC* Program
## Day 1  (Week 1): **Change of Direction**

### Warm up activity

| Exercise | Reps | Sets | Tempo | Rest Interval |
|---|---|---|---|---|
| Active Warm Up Exercise (Skips, Butt kicks, etc..) | 20 yards per | 1 | Moderate Pace | <10s per exercise |
| Postural Correction Exercises | 20-40 per exercise | 1 | Controlled or Static | <30s per exercise |
| Hip Mobility Circuit | 10-15 per | 1 | Controlled | Done in Circuit Fashion |

### Jumping Exercises

| Exercise | Set | Reps | Rest Interval |
|---|---|---|---|
| 1. Single Leg Broad Jump | 4 | 6 | 60s. |
| 2. Horizontal to vertical (pushup to jump to feet) broad/high jump with full hip extension | 3 | 4 | 60s |
| 3. Skater hops with 2s stick the landing | 3 | 6 | 60s |
| 4. Power skips for distance (try to cover 30yds) | 4 | 6 reps (try to cover 30yds) | 60s |
| 5. Change of direction single leg reactive broad jump | 4 | 6 (3 per side) | 60s |

### Change of Direction Sprints and Agility

| Exercise | Set | Reps | Rest Interval |
|---|---|---|---|
| 1. T-Drill (10-5-10-5-10) | 6 | 1 | 40s. |
| 2. Teams of 5, 5 yard wide 5 yard deep slalom sprints | 2 | 100yds | 120s |

227

## *EA* Football *SAC* Program
## Day 2  (Week 1): **Hill Sprints**

### Warm up activity

| Exercise | Reps | Sets | Tempo | Rest Interval |
|---|---|---|---|---|
| Active Warm Up Exercise (Skips, Butt kicks, etc..) | 20 yards per | 1 | Moderate Pace | <10s per exercise |
| Postural Correction Exercises | 20-40 per exercise | 1 | Controlled or Static | <30s per exercise |
| Hip Mobility Circuit | 10-15 per | 1 | Controlled | Done in Circuit Fashion |

### Hill Sprints

| Exercise | Set | Reps | Rest Interval |
|---|---|---|---|
| 1. 20 Yard Hill Accelerations from 3 point stance | 4 | 1 | 50s. |
| 2. 40 Yard Timed Hill Sprint | 4 | 1 (set baseline time; times will be dependent on grade of hill) | 60s |
| 3. 60 Yard Timed Hill Sprint | 2 | 1 (set baseline time; times will be dependent on grade of hill) | 90s |
| 4. Finisher: Bear Crawl up/jog down/backward run up/jog down | 1 | 1 | |

# *EA* Football *SAC* Program
## Day 3  (Week 1): **Field Sprints**
### Warm up activity

| Exercise | Reps | Sets | Tempo | Rest Interval |
|----------|------|------|-------|---------------|
| Active Warm Up Exercise (Skips, Butt kicks, etc..) | 20 yards per | 1 | Moderate Pace | <10s per exercise |
| Postural Correction Exercises | 20-40 per exercise | 1 | Controlled or Static | <30s per exercise |
| Hip Mobility Circuit | 10-15 per | 1 | Controlled | Done in Circuit Fashion |

### Resisted Sprints/Accelerations

| Exercise | Set | Reps | Rest Interval |
|----------|-----|------|---------------|
| 1. 15yds | 4 | 1 | 60s. |
| 2. 20yds | 3 | 1 | 60s |

### Field Sprints

| Exercise | Set | Reps | Rest Interval |
|----------|-----|------|---------------|
| 1. 5-Goal Line-10yd change of direction sprint | 2 | 2 (1 each side) | 30s. |
| 2. 10-Goal Line- 20yd change of direction sprint | 1 | 2 (1 each side) | 30s |
| 3. Timed 40 yd sprint from 3 point start | 4 | 1 (skill <5.5s/Lineman <7s) | 60s |
| 4. 60 yd sprint | 1 | 1 | 60s |
| 5. Timed 80 yd sprint | 2 | 1 (skill <10.5s/Lineman <13s) | 60s |
| 6. Finisher: 200 Shuttle | 1 | 1 (skill < 30s/ Lineman < 38s) | NA |

# Week 2

## EA Football *SAC* Program
## Day 1  (Week 2): **Change of Direction**

### Warm up activity

| Exercise | Reps | Sets | Tempo | Rest Interval |
|---|---|---|---|---|
| Active Warm Up Exercise (Skips, Butt kicks, etc..) | 20 yards per | 1 | Moderate Pace | <10s per exercise |
| Postural Correction Exercises | 20-40 per exercise | 1 | Controlled or Static | <30s per exercise |
| Hip Mobility Circuit | 10-15 per | 1 | Controlled | Done in Circuit Fashion |

### Jumping Exercises

| Exercise | Set | Reps | Rest Interval |
|---|---|---|---|
| 1. Single Leg Broad Jump | 4 | 6 | 60s. |
| 2. Horizontal to vertical (pushup to jump to feet) broad/high jump with full hip extension | 3 | 4 | 60s |
| 3. Skater hops with 2s stick the landing | 3 | 6 | 60s |
| 4. Power skips for distance (try to cover 30yds) | 4 | 6 reps (try to cover 30yds) | 60s |
| 5. Change of direction single leg reactive broad jump | 4 | 6 (3 per side) | 60s |

### Change of Direction Sprints and Agility

| Exercise | Set | Reps | Rest Interval |
|---|---|---|---|
| 1. T-Drill (10-5-10-5-10) | 6 | 1 | 40s. |
| 2. Teams of 5, 5 yard wide 5 yard deep slalom sprints | 2 | 100yds | 110s |

231

# *EA* Football *SAC* Program
## Day 2  (Week 2): **Hill Sprints**

### Warm up activity

| Exercise | Reps | Sets | Tempo | Rest Interval |
|---|---|---|---|---|
| Active Warm Up Exercise (Skips, Butt kicks, etc..) | 20 yards per | 1 | Moderate Pace | <10s per exercise |
| Postural Correction Exercises | 20-40 per exercise | 1 | Controlled or Static | <30s per exercise |
| Hip Mobility Circuit | 10-15 per | 1 | Controlled | Done in Circuit Fashion |

### Hill Sprints

| Exercise | Set | Reps | Rest Interval |
|---|---|---|---|
| 1. 20 Yard Hill Accelerations from 3 point stance | 4 | 1 | 50s. |
| 2. 40 Yard Timed Hill Sprint | 4 | 1 (set baseline time; times will be dependent on grade of hill) | 60s |
| 3. 60 Yard Timed Hill Sprint | 3 | 1 (set baseline time; times will be dependent on grade of hill) | 80s |
| 4. Finisher: Bear Crawl up/jog down/backward run up/jog down | 1 | 1 | |

# *EA* Football *SAC* Program
## Day 3  (Week 2): **Field Sprints**
## Warm up activity

| Exercise | Reps | Sets | Tempo | Rest Interval |
|---|---|---|---|---|
| Active Warm Up Exercise (Skips, Butt kicks, etc..) | 20 yards per | 1 | Moderate Pace | <10s per exercise |
| Postural Correction Exercises | 20-40 per exercise | 1 | Controlled or Static | <30s per exercise |
| Hip Mobility Circuit | 10-15 per | 1 | Controlled | Done in Circuit Fashion |

## Resisted Sprints/Accelerations

| Exercise | Set | Reps | Rest Interval |
|---|---|---|---|
| 1. 15yds | 4 | 1 | 50s. |
| 2. 20yds | 4 | 1 | 50s |

## Field Sprints

| Exercise | Set | Reps | Rest Interval |
|---|---|---|---|
| 1. 5-Goal Line-10yd change of direction sprint | 2 | 2 (1 each side) | 30s. |
| 2. 10-Goal Line- 20yd change of direction sprint | 1 | 2 (1 each side) | 30s |
| 3. Timed 40 yd sprint from 3 point start | 4 | 1 (skill <5.5s/Lineman <7s) | 60s |
| 4. 60 yd sprint | 1 | 1 | 60s |
| 5. Timed 80 yd sprint | 2 | 1 (skill <10.5s/Lineman <13s) | 60s |
| 6. Finisher: 200 Shuttle | 1 | 1 (skill < 30s/ Lineman < 38s) | NA |

# Week 3

## *EA* Football *SAC* Program

## Day 1  (Week 3): **Change of Direction**

### Warm up activity

| Exercise | Reps | Sets | Tempo | Rest Interval |
|---|---|---|---|---|
| Active Warm Up Exercise (Skips, Butt kicks, etc..) | 20 yards per | 1 | Moderate Pace | <10s per exercise |
| Postural Correction Exercises | 20-40 per exercise | 1 | Controlled or Static | <30s per exercise |
| Hip Mobility Circuit | 10-15 per | 1 | Controlled | Done in Circuit Fashion |

### Jumping Exercises

| Exercise | Set | Reps | Rest Interval |
|---|---|---|---|
| 1. Single Leg Broad Jump | 4 | 6 | 60s. |
| 2. Horizontal to vertical (pushup to jump to feet) broad/high jump with full hip extension | 3 | 4 | 60s |
| 3. Skater hops with 2s stick the landing | 3 | 6 | 60s |
| 4. Power skips for distance (try to cover 30yds) | 4 | 6 reps (try to cover 30yds) | 60s |
| 5. Change of direction single leg reactive broad jump | 4 | 6 (3 per side) | 60s |

### Change of Direction Sprints and Agility

| Exercise | Set | Reps | Rest Interval |
|---|---|---|---|
| 1. T-Drill (10-5-10-5-10) | 6 | 1 | 40s. |
| 2. Teams of 5, 5 yard wide 5 yard deep slalom sprints | 2 | 100yds | 100s |

235

# *EA* Football *SAC* Program
## Day 2  (Week 3): **Hill Sprints**

### Warm up activity

| Exercise | Reps | Sets | Tempo | Rest Interval |
|---|---|---|---|---|
| Active Warm Up Exercise (Skips, Butt kicks, etc..) | 20 yards per | 1 | Moderate Pace | <10s per exercise |
| Postural Correction Exercises | 20-40 per exercise | 1 | Controlled or Static | <30s per exercise |
| Hip Mobility Circuit | 10-15 per | 1 | Controlled | Done in Circuit Fashion |

### Hill Sprints

| Exercise | Set | Reps | Rest Interval |
|---|---|---|---|
| 1. 20 Yard Hill Accelerations from 3 point stance | 5 | 1 | 45s. |
| 2. 40 Yard Timed Hill Sprint | 5 | 1 (set baseline time; times will be dependent on grade of hill) | 50s |
| 3. 60 Yard Timed Hill Sprint | 3 | 1 (set baseline time; times will be dependent on grade of hill) | 80s |
| 4. Finisher: Bear Crawl up/jog down/backward run up/jog down | 1 | 1 | |

# *EA* Football *SAC* Program
## Day 3  (Week 3): **Field Sprints**
### Warm up activity

| Exercise | Reps | Sets | Tempo | Rest Interval |
|---|---|---|---|---|
| Active Warm Up Exercise (Skips, Butt kicks, etc..) | 20 yards per | 1 | Moderate Pace | <10s per exercise |
| Postural Correction Exercises | 20-40 per exercise | 1 | Controlled or Static | <30s per exercise |
| Hip Mobility Circuit | 10-15 per | 1 | Controlled | Done in Circuit Fashion |

### Resisted Sprints/Accelerations

| Exercise | Set | Reps | Rest Interval |
|---|---|---|---|
| 1. 15yds | 5 | 1 | 50s. |
| 2. 20yds | 4 | 1 | 50s |

### Field Sprints

| Exercise | Set | Reps | Rest Interval |
|---|---|---|---|
| 1. 5-Goal Line-10yd change of direction sprint | 2 | 2 (1 each side) | 30s. |
| 2. 10-Goal Line- 20yd change of direction sprint | 1 | 2 (1 each side) | 30s |
| 3. Timed 40 yd sprint from 3 point start | 5 | 1 (skill <5.5s/Lineman <7s) | 60s |
| 4. 60 yd sprint | 2 | 1 | 60s |
| 5. Timed 80 yd sprint | 2 | 1 (skill <10.5s/Lineman <13s) | 60s |
| 6. Finisher: 200 Shuttle | 1 | 1 (skill < 30s/ Lineman < 38s) | NA |

237

# Week 4

## *EA* Football *SAC* Program

## Day 1  (Week 4): **Change of Direction**

### Warm up activity

| Exercise | Reps | Sets | Tempo | Rest Interval |
|---|---|---|---|---|
| Active Warm Up Exercise (Skips, Butt kicks, etc..) | 20 yards per | 1 | Moderate Pace | <10s per exercise |
| Postural Correction Exercises | 20-40 per exercise | 1 | Controlled or Static | <30s per exercise |
| Hip Mobility Circuit | 10-15 per | 1 | Controlled | Done in Circuit Fashion |

### Jumping Exercises

| Exercise | Set | Reps | Rest Interval |
|---|---|---|---|
| 1. Single Leg Broad Jump | 4 | 6 | 50s. |
| 2. Horizontal to vertical (pushup to jump to feet) broad/high jump with full hip extension | 4 | 4 | 50s |
| 3. Skater hops with 2s stick the landing | 3 | 6 | 50s |
| 4. Power skips for distance (try to cover 30yds) | 4 | 6 reps (try to cover 30yds) | 50s |
| 5. Change of direction single leg reactive broad jump | 4 | 6 (3 per side) | 50s |

### Change of Direction Sprints and Agility

| Exercise | Set | Reps | Rest Interval |
|---|---|---|---|
| 1. T-Drill (10-5-10-5-10) | 6 | 1 | 40s. |
| 2. Teams of 5, 5 yard wide 5 yard deep slalom sprints | 3 | 100yds | 110s |

239

# *EA* Football *SAC* Program
## Day 2  (Week 4): **Hill Sprints**

### Warm up activity

| Exercise | Reps | Sets | Tempo | Rest Interval |
|---|---|---|---|---|
| Active Warm Up Exercise (Skips, Butt kicks, etc..) | 20 yards per | 1 | Moderate Pace | <10s per exercise |
| Postural Correction Exercises | 20-40 per exercise | 1 | Controlled or Static | <30s per exercise |
| Hip Mobility Circuit | 10-15 per | 1 | Controlled | Done in Circuit Fashion |

### Hill Sprints

| Exercise | Set | Reps | Rest Interval |
|---|---|---|---|
| 1. 20 Yard Hill Accelerations from 3 point stance | 5 | 1 | 45s. |
| 2. 40 Yard Timed Hill Sprint | 5 | 1 (set baseline time; times will be dependent on grade of hill) | 50s |
| 3. 60 Yard Timed Hill Sprint | 3 | 1 (set baseline time; times will be dependent on grade of hill) | 70s |
| 4. Finisher: Bear Crawl up/jog down/backward run up/jog down | 2 | 1 | |

# *EA* Football *SAC* Program
## Day 3   (Week 4): **Field Sprints**
### Warm up activity

| Exercise | Reps | Sets | Tempo | Rest Interval |
|---|---|---|---|---|
| Active Warm Up Exercise (Skips, Butt kicks, etc..) | 20 yards per | 1 | Moderate Pace | <10s per exercise |
| Postural Correction Exercises | 20-40 per exercise | 1 | Controlled or Static | <30s per exercise |
| Hip Mobility Circuit | 10-15 per | 1 | Controlled | Done in Circuit Fashion |

### Resisted Sprints/Accelerations

| Exercise | Set | Reps | Rest Interval |
|---|---|---|---|
| 1. 15yds | 5 | 1 | 50s. |
| 2. 20yds | 5 | 1 | 50s |

### Field Sprints

| Exercise | Set | Reps | Rest Interval |
|---|---|---|---|
| 1. 5-Goal Line-10yd change of direction sprint | 2 | 2 (1 each side) | 30s. |
| 2. 10-Goal Line- 20yd change of direction sprint | 2 | 2 (1 each side) | 30s |
| 3. Timed 40 yd sprint from 3 point start | 5 | 1 (skill <5.5s/Lineman <7s) | 60s |
| 4. 60 yd sprint | 2 | 1 | 60s |
| 5. Timed 80 yd sprint | 3 | 1 (skill <10.5s/Lineman <13s) | 60s |
| 6. Finisher: 200 Shuttle | 1 | 1 (skill < 30s/ Lineman < 38s) | NA |

# Week 5 Low Volume Week
## *EA* Football *SAC* Program
## Day 1  (Week 5): **Change of Direction Low Volume**

## Warm up activity

| Exercise | Reps | Sets | Tempo | Rest Interval |
|---|---|---|---|---|
| Active Warm Up Exercise (Skips, Butt kicks, etc..) | 20 yards per | 1 | Moderate Pace | <10s per exercise |
| Postural Correction Exercises | 20-40 per exercise | 1 | Controlled or Static | <30s per exercise |
| Hip Mobility Circuit | 10-15 per | 1 | Controlled | Done in Circuit Fashion |

## Jumping Exercises

| Exercise | Set | Reps | Rest Interval |
|---|---|---|---|
| 1. Single Leg Broad Jump | 2 | 6 | 60s. |
| 2. Horizontal to vertical (pushup to jump to feet) broad/high jump with full hip extension | 1 | 4 | 60s |
| 3. Skater hops with 2s stick the landing | 0 | 0 | 60s |
| 4. Power skips for distance (try to cover 30yds) | 2 | 6 reps (try to cover 30yds) | 60s |
| 5. Change of direction single leg reactive broad jump | 2 | 6 (3 per side) | 60s |

## Change of Direction Sprints and Agility

| Exercise | Set | Reps | Rest Interval |
|---|---|---|---|
| 1. T-Drill (10-5-10-5-10) | 2 | 1 | 40s. |
| 2. Teams of 5, 5 yard wide 5 yard deep slalom sprints | 0 | 0 | 120s |

243

# *EA* Football *SAC* Program
## Day 2  (Week 5): **Hill Sprints Low Volume**

### Warm up activity

| Exercise | Reps | Sets | Tempo | Rest Interval |
|---|---|---|---|---|
| Active Warm Up Exercise (Skips, Butt kicks, etc..) | 20 yards per | 1 | Moderate Pace | <10s per exercise |
| Postural Correction Exercises | 20-40 per exercise | 1 | Controlled or Static | <30s per exercise |
| Hip Mobility Circuit | 10-15 per | 1 | Controlled | Done in Circuit Fashion |

### Hill Sprints

| Exercise | Set | Reps | Rest Interval |
|---|---|---|---|
| 1. 20 Yard Hill Accelerations from 3 point stance | 2 | 1 | 50s. |
| 2. 40 Yard Timed Hill Sprint | 2 | 1 (set baseline time; times will be dependent on grade of hill) | 60s |
| 3. 60 Yard Timed Hill Sprint | 2 | 1 (set baseline time; times will be dependent on grade of hill) | 90s |
| 4. Finisher: Bear Crawl up/jog down/backward run up/jog down | 0 | 0 | |

# *EA* Football *SAC* Program
## Day 3  (Week 5): **Field Sprints Low Volume**
### Warm up activity

| Exercise | Reps | Sets | Tempo | Rest Interval |
|---|---|---|---|---|
| Active Warm Up Exercise (Skips, Butt kicks, etc..) | 20 yards per | 1 | Moderate Pace | <10s per exercise |
| Postural Correction Exercises | 20-40 per exercise | 1 | Controlled or Static | <30s per exercise |
| Hip Mobility Circuit | 10-15 per | 1 | Controlled | Done in Circuit Fashion |

### Resisted Sprints/Accelerations

| Exercise | Set | Reps | Rest Interval |
|---|---|---|---|
| 1. 15yds | 2 | 1 | 50s. |
| 2. 20yds | 2 | 1 | 50s |

### Field Sprints

| Exercise | Set | Reps | Rest Interval |
|---|---|---|---|
| 1. 5-Goal Line-10yd change of direction sprint | 1 | 2 (1 each side) | 30s. |
| 2. 10-Goal Line- 20yd change of direction sprint | 1 | 2 (1 each side) | 30s |
| 3. Timed 40 yd sprint from 3 point start | 2 | 1 (skill <5.5s/Lineman <7s) | 60s |
| 4. 60 yd sprint | 0 | 1 | 60s |
| 5. Timed 80 yd sprint | 1 | 1 (skill <10.5s/Lineman <13s) | 60s |
| 6. Finisher: 200 Shuttle | 0 | 1 (skill < 30s/ Lineman < 38s) | NA |

# Week 6
## *EA* Football *SAC* Program
## Day 1  (Week 6): **Change of Direction**

### Warm up activity

| Exercise | Reps | Sets | Tempo | Rest Interval |
|---|---|---|---|---|
| Active Warm Up Exercise (Skips, Butt kicks, etc..) | 20 yards per | 1 | Moderate Pace | <10s per exercise |
| Postural Correction Exercises | 20-40 per exercise | 1 | Controlled or Static | <30s per exercise |
| Hip Mobility Circuit | 10-15 per | 1 | Controlled | Done in Circuit Fashion |

### Jumping Exercises

| Exercise | Set | Reps | Rest Interval |
|---|---|---|---|
| 1. Single Leg Broad Jump | 4 | 6 | 45s. |
| 2. Horizontal to vertical (pushup to jump to feet) broad/high jump with full hip extension | 4 | 4 | 45s |
| 3. Skater hops with 2s stick the landing | 3 | 6 | 45s |
| 4. Power skips for distance (try to cover 30yds) | 4 | 6 reps (try to cover 30yds) | 45s |
| 5. Change of direction single leg reactive broad jump | 4 | 6 (3 per side) | 45s |

### Change of Direction Sprints and Agility

| Exercise | Set | Reps | Rest Interval |
|---|---|---|---|
| 1. T-Drill (10-5-10-5-10) | 6 | 1 | 40s. |
| 2. Teams of 5, 5 yard wide 5 yard deep slalom sprints | 3 | 100yds | 100s |

247

# *EA* Football *SAC* Program
## Day 2  (Week 6): **Hill Sprints**

## Warm up activity

| Exercise | Reps | Sets | Tempo | Rest Interval |
|---|---|---|---|---|
| Active Warm Up Exercise (Skips, Butt kicks, etc..) | 20 yards per | 1 | Moderate Pace | <10s per exercise |
| Postural Correction Exercises | 20-40 per exercise | 1 | Controlled or Static | <30s per exercise |
| Hip Mobility Circuit | 10-15 per | 1 | Controlled | Done in Circuit Fashion |

## Hill Sprints

| Exercise | Set | Reps | Rest Interval |
|---|---|---|---|
| 1. 20 Yard Hill Accelerations from 3 point stance | 5 | 1 | 45s. |
| 2. 40 Yard Timed Hill Sprint | 5 | 1 (set baseline time; times will be dependent on grade of hill) | 45s |
| 3. 60 Yard Timed Hill Sprint | 4 | 1 (set baseline time; times will be dependent on grade of hill) | 60s |
| 4. Finisher: Bear Crawl up/jog down/backward run up/jog down | 2 | 1 | |

# *EA* Football *SAC* Program
## Day 3  (Week 6): **Field Sprints**
### Warm up activity

| Exercise | Reps | Sets | Tempo | Rest Interval |
|---|---|---|---|---|
| Active Warm Up Exercise (Skips, Butt kicks, etc..) | 20 yards per | 1 | Moderate Pace | <10s per exercise |
| Postural Correction Exercises | 20-40 per exercise | 1 | Controlled or Static | <30s per exercise |
| Hip Mobility Circuit | 10-15 per | 1 | Controlled | Done in Circuit Fashion |

### Resisted Sprints/Accelerations

| Exercise | Set | Reps | Rest Interval |
|---|---|---|---|
| 1. 15yds | 5 | 1 | 50s. |
| 2. 20yds | 5 | 1 | 50s |

### Field Sprints

| Exercise | Set | Reps | Rest Interval |
|---|---|---|---|
| 1. 5-Goal Line-10yd change of direction sprint | 2 | 2 (1 each side) | 30s. |
| 2. 10-Goal Line- 20yd change of direction sprint | 2 | 2 (1 each side) | 30s |
| 3. Timed 40 yd sprint from 3 point start | 6 | 1 (skill <5.5s/Lineman <7s) | 60s |
| 4. 60 yd sprint | 2 | 1 | 60s |
| 5. Timed 80 yd sprint | 4 | 1 (skill <10.5s/Lineman <13s) | 60s |
| 6. Finisher: 200 Shuttle | 1 | 1 (skill < 30s/ Lineman < 38s) | NA |

# Week 7

## *EA* Football *SAC* Program
## Day 1  (Week 7): **Change of Direction**

### Warm up activity

| Exercise | Reps | Sets | Tempo | Rest Interval |
|---|---|---|---|---|
| Active Warm Up Exercise (Skips, Butt kicks, etc..) | 20 yards per | 1 | Moderate Pace | <10s per exercise |
| Postural Correction Exercises | 20-40 per exercise | 1 | Controlled or Static | <30s per exercise |
| Hip Mobility Circuit | 10-15 per | 1 | Controlled | Done in Circuit Fashion |

### Jumping Exercises

| Exercise | Set | Reps | Rest Interval |
|---|---|---|---|
| 1. Single Leg Broad Jump | 4 | 6 | 40s. |
| 2. Horizontal to vertical (pushup to jump to feet) broad/high jump with full hip extension | 4 | 4 | 40s |
| 3. Skater hops with 2s stick the landing | 3 | 6 | 40s |
| 4. Power skips for distance (try to cover 30yds) | 4 | 6 reps (try to cover 30yds) | 40s |
| 5. Change of direction single leg reactive broad jump | 4 | 6 (3 per side) | 40s |

### Change of Direction Sprints and Agility

| Exercise | Set | Reps | Rest Interval |
|---|---|---|---|
| 1. T-Drill (10-5-10-5-10) | 6 | 1 | 40s. |
| 2. Teams of 5, 5 yard wide 5 yard deep slalom sprints | 3 | 100yds | 90s |

## *EA* Football *SAC* Program
## Day 2  (Week 7): **Hill Sprints**

### Warm up activity

| Exercise | Reps | Sets | Tempo | Rest Interval |
|---|---|---|---|---|
| Active Warm Up Exercise (Skips, Butt kicks, etc..) | 20 yards per | 1 | Moderate Pace | <10s per exercise |
| Postural Correction Exercises | 20-40 per exercise | 1 | Controlled or Static | <30s per exercise |
| Hip Mobility Circuit | 10-15 per | 1 | Controlled | Done in Circuit Fashion |

### Hill Sprints

| Exercise | Set | Reps | Rest Interval |
|---|---|---|---|
| 1. 20 Yard Hill Accelerations from 3 point stance | 6 | 1 | 40s. |
| 2. 40 Yard Timed Hill Sprint | 6 | 1 (set baseline time; times will be dependent on grade of hill) | 40s |
| 3. 60 Yard Timed Hill Sprint | 5 | 1 (set baseline time; times will be dependent on grade of hill) | 50s |
| 4. Finisher: Bear Crawl up/jog down/backward run up/jog down | 2 | 1 | |

## *EA* Football *SAC* Program
## Day 3  (Week 7): **Field Sprints**
## Warm up activity

| Exercise | Reps | Sets | Tempo | Rest Interval |
|---|---|---|---|---|
| Active Warm Up Exercise (Skips, Butt kicks, etc..) | 20 yards per | 1 | Moderate Pace | <10s per exercise |
| Postural Correction Exercises | 20-40 per exercise | 1 | Controlled or Static | <30s per exercise |
| Hip Mobility Circuit | 10-15 per | 1 | Controlled | Done in Circuit Fashion |

## Resisted Sprints/Accelerations

| Exercise | Set | Reps | Rest Interval |
|---|---|---|---|
| 1. 15yds | 5 | 1 | 50s. |
| 2. 20yds | 5 | 1 | 50s |

## Field Sprints

| Exercise | Set | Reps | Rest Interval |
|---|---|---|---|
| 1. 5-Goal Line-10yd change of direction sprint | 2 | 2 (1 each side) | 30s. |
| 2. 10-Goal Line- 20yd change of direction sprint | 2 | 2 (1 each side) | 30s |
| 3. Timed 40 yd sprint from 3 point start | 7 | 1 (skill <5.5s/Lineman <7s) | 60s |
| 4. 60 yd sprint | 2 | 1 | 60s |
| 5. Timed 80 yd sprint | 5 | 1 (skill <10.5s/Lineman <13s) | 60s |
| 6. Finisher: 200 Shuttle | 1 | 1 (skill < 30s/ Lineman < 38s) | NA |

# Week 8

## *EA* Football *SAC* Program
## Day 1  (Week 8): **Change of Direction**

### Warm up activity

| Exercise | Reps | Sets | Tempo | Rest Interval |
|---|---|---|---|---|
| Active Warm Up Excrcise (Skips, Butt kicks, etc..) | 20 yards per | 1 | Moderate Pace | <10s per exercise |
| Postural Correction Exercises | 20-40 per exercise | 1 | Controlled or Static | <30s per exercise |
| Hip Mobility Circuit | 10-15 per | 1 | Controlled | Done in Circuit Fashion |

### Jumping Exercises

| Exercise | Set | Reps | Rest Interval |
|---|---|---|---|
| 1. Single Leg Broad Jump | 4 | 6 | 40s. |
| 2. Horizontal to vertical (pushup to jump to feet) broad/high jump with full hip extension | 4 | 4 | 40s |
| 3. Skater hops with 2s stick the landing | 3 | 6 | 40s |
| 4. Power skips for distance (try to cover 30yds) | 4 | 6 reps (try to cover 30yds) | 40s |
| 5. Change of direction single leg reactive broad jump | 4 | 6 (3 per side) | 40s |

### Change of Direction Sprints and Agility

| Exercise | Set | Reps | Rest Interval |
|---|---|---|---|
| 1. T-Drill (10-5-10-5-10) | 6 | 1 | 40s. |
| 2. Teams of 5, 5 yard wide 5 yard deep slalom sprints | 1 | 100yds | NA |

255

# *EA* Football *SAC* Program
## Day 2  (Week 8): **Hill Sprints**

### Warm up activity

| Exercise | Reps | Sets | Tempo | Rest Interval |
|---|---|---|---|---|
| Active Warm Up Exercise (Skips, Butt kicks, etc..) | 20 yards per | 1 | Moderate Pace | <10s per exercise |
| Postural Correction Exercises | 20-40 per exercise | 1 | Controlled or Static | <30s per exercise |
| Hip Mobility Circuit | 10-15 per | 1 | Controlled | Done in Circuit Fashion |

### Hill Sprints

| Exercise | Set | Reps | Rest Interval |
|---|---|---|---|
| 1. 20 Yard Hill Accelerations from 3 point stance | 2 | 1 | 40s. |
| 2. 40 Yard Timed Hill Sprint | 2 | 1 (set baseline time; times will be dependent on grade of hill) | 40s |
| 3. 60 Yard Timed Hill Sprint | 2 | 1 (set baseline time; times will be dependent on grade of hill) | 50s |
| 4. Finisher: Bear Crawl up/jog down/backward run up/jog down | 1 | 1 | |

# *EA* Football *SAC* Program
## Day 3  (Week 8): **Field Sprints Low Volume**
### Warm up activity

| Exercise | Reps | Sets | Tempo | Rest Interval |
|---|---|---|---|---|
| Active Warm Up Exercise (Skips, Butt kicks, etc..) | 20 yards per | 1 | Moderate Pace | <10s per exercise |
| Postural Correction Exercises | 20-40 per exercise | 1 | Controlled or Static | <30s per exercise |
| Hip Mobility Circuit | 10-15 per | 1 | Controlled | Done in Circuit Fashion |

### Resisted Sprints/Accelerations

| Exercise | Set | Reps | Rest Interval |
|---|---|---|---|
| 1. 15yds | 6 | 1 | 50s. |
| 2. 20yds | 6 | 1 | 50s |

### Field Sprints

| Exercise | Set | Reps | Rest Interval |
|---|---|---|---|
| 1. 5-Goal Line-10yd change of direction sprint | 2 | 2 (1 each side) | 30s. |
| 2. 10-Goal Line- 20yd change of direction sprint | 2 | 2 (1 each side) | 30s |
| 3. Timed 40 yd sprint from 3 point start | 2 | 1 (skill <5.5s/Lineman <7s) | 60s |
| 4. 60 yd sprint | 1 | 1 | 60s |
| 5. Timed 80 yd sprint | 2 | 1 (skill <10.5s/Lineman <13s) | 60s |
| 6. Finisher: 200 Shuttle | 1 | 1 (skill < 30s/ Lineman < 38s) | NA |

**Closing thoughts:**

As you have seen, there are many ways to improve an athlete's acceleration. Whether it be immediate or long term gains, factors including rest periods, training age, exercise selection, reps, clustered sets, accommodating resistance, contrast or complex methods, overhead goal training, uneven surface training, Olympic lifts, sled pushes and pulls, modified strongman training, recovery methods, etc, the goal is the same: Improve movement quality and add more horsepower to the motor.

Going back to the 2006 personal conversation about scholarships with the top 10 college football program recruiting director we mentioned at the beginning of this book.

> *1. How high an athlete can jump.*
>
> *2. How the athlete treats their mother.*

The brilliance of that answer lies in its straight to the point simplicity. How high an athlete can jump is reflective of how well they move and how quickly they can generate force or accelerate. For most athletes this is a result of two main things: genetics and how hard they have worked.

The second thing he looked for "how an athlete treats their mother" is a lesson in character and the humility, respect, and coachability that comes from all those hours spent on the field and in the weight room. Oftentimes, on any team, the hardest workers just so happen to be the best leaders/players.

Thank you for picking up a copy of this book. It has been our honor and pleasure to have you take the time to read it. We hope you enjoyed it and are able to use some of the information to your personal or team's benefit. We would greatly appreciate if you could take a minute to write a quick review on Amazon.com as your feedback is important to us.

Stay tuned for future books in our Specific Sports Training and Athletic Workout Programs Series!

Other books in the series include: *(click on the book for the link)*

Other books by Jason Shea include the Healthy Aging For Busy

Parents and Professionals Series.

### Book 1

### Book 2

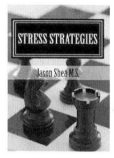

### Book 3

### Book 4

# References

## Chapter I

1. Bret et al. **Leg strength and stiffness as ability factors in 100 m sprint running**. *Journal of Sports Medicine and Physical Fitness*. 42; Pp 274-281. 2002.
2. Brown J et al. **Back pain in a large Canadian police force**. *Spine*. 23(7); Pp 821-827. 1998.
3. Daveena S et al. **Lower-Body Power Relationships to Linear Speed, Change-of-Direction Speed, and High-Intensity Running Performance in DI Collegiate Women's Basketball Players**. *Journal of Human Kinetics*. 68; Pp 223-232. 2019.
4. Delaney et al. **Contributing factors to change-of-direction ability in professional rugby league players**. *Journal of Strength and Conditioning Research*. 29; Pp 2688-2696. 2015.
5. Lockie et al. **Factors that differentiate acceleration ability in field sport athletes**. *Journal of Strength and Conditioning Research*. 25; Pp 2704-2714. 2011.
6. Lockie et al. **Relationship between unilateral jumping ability and asymmetry on multidirectional speed in team-sport athletes**. *Journal of Strength and Conditioning Research*. 28; Pp 3557-3566. 2014.
7. Lockie R, et al. **Relationships and Predictive Capabilities of Jump Assessments to Soccer-Specific Field Test Performance in Division I Collegiate Players**. *Sports (Basel)*. 4(4); Pp 56. 2016.
8. Loturco et al. **Vertical and horizontal jump tests are strongly associated with competitive performance in 100-m dash events**. *Journal of Strength and Conditioning Research*. 29; Pp 1966-1971. 2015.
9. McCurdy et al. **The relationship between kinematic determinants of jump and sprint performance in Division I women soccer players**. *Journal of Strength and Conditioning Research*. 24; Pp 3200-3208. 2010.
10. McFarland et al. **Relationship of two vertical jumping tests to sprint and change of direction speed among male and female collegiate soccer players**. *Sports*. 4; 2016.
11. Myer G et al. **The effects of generalized joint laxity on risk of anterior cruciate ligament injury in young female athletes**. *American Journal of Sports Medicine*. 36(6); Pp 1073-1080. 2008.
12. Parkkari J et al. **The risk for a cruciate ligament injury of the knee in adolescents and young adults: a population-based cohort study of 46,500 people with a 9 year follow-up**. *British Journal of Medicine*. 42(6); Pp 422-426. 2008.

13. Sekulic et al. **Gender-specific influences of balance, speed, and power on agility performance**. *Journal of Strength and Conditioning Research*. 27; Pp 802-811. 2013.

## Chapter 2

1. Alcaraz et al. **The Effectiveness of Resisted Sled Training (RST) for Sprint Performance: A Systematic Review and Meta-analysis.** *Sports Medicine*. 48(9); Pp 2143-2165. 2018.
2. Bauer et al. **Combining higher-load and lower-load resistance training exercises: A systematic review and meta-analysis of findings from complex training studies.** *J Sci Med Sports*. 22(7); Pp 838-851. 2019.
3. Bevan et al. **Influence of postactivation potentiation on sprinting performance in professional rugby players.** *Journal of Strength and Conditioning Research*. 24(3); Pp 701-705. 2010.
4. Cahill et al. **Sled-Pull Load–Velocity Profiling and Implications for Sprint Training Prescription in Young Male Athletes.** *Sports*. 7, 119; doi:10.3390/sports7050119. 2019.
5. Cahill et al. **Influence of resisted sled-push training on the sprint force-velocity profile of male high school athletes.** *Scandinavian Journal of Medicine and Science in Sports*. 30(3); Pp 442-449. 2020.
6. Cahill et al. **Sled-Push Load-Velocity Profiling and Implications for Sprint Training Prescription in Young Athletes**. *Journal of Strength and Conditioning Research*. 2020.
7. Comfort et al. **Relationships between strength, sprint, and jump performance in well-trained youth soccer players.** *The Journal of Strength and Conditioning Research*. 28(1); Pp 173-177. 2014.
8. Cormier et al. **Complex and Contrast Training: Does Strength and Power Training Sequence Affect Performance-Based Adaptations in Team Sports? A Systematic Review and Meta-analysis.** *Journal of Strength and Conditioning Research*. 2020.
9. Cross et al. **A comparison between the force-velocity relationships of unloaded and sled-resisted sprinting: single vs. multiple trial methods.** *European Journal of Applied Physiology*. 118; Pp 563–571. 2018.
10. Cronin et al. **Strength and Power Predictors of Sports Speed.** *The Journal of Strength and Conditioning Research*. 19(2); Pp 349-357. 2005.
11. de Hoyo et al. **Comparative Effects of In-Season Full-Back Squat, Resisted Sprint Training, and Plyometric Training on Explosive**

Performance in U-19 Elite Soccer Players. *Journal of Strength and Conditioning Research*. 30(2); Pp 368-377. 2016.

12. DeWeese et al. **Sliding toward Sochi-part I: A review of programming tactics used during the 2010 - 2014 quadrennial.** *NSCA Coach*. 1(3); Pp 30-32. 2014.

13. Elbadry et al. **Effect of the French Contrast Method on Explosive Strength and Kinematic Parameters of the Triple Jump Among Female College Athletes.** *Journal of Human Kinetics*. 69; Pp 225-230. 2019.

14. Frolov et al. **Block Organization of Training Load of Elite Bobsledders in a Year Training Cycle.** *Russian State University of Physical Culture, Sport, Youth, and Tourism*.

15. Harrison A. **The Bobsled Push Start: Influence on Race Outcome and Push Athlete Talent Identification and Monitoring.** *Electronic Theses and Dissertations. Paper 3313. https://dc.etsu.edu/etd/3313. East Tennessee State University*. 2017.

16. Hartmann H, Wirth K, Klusemann M. **Analysis of the load on the knee joint and vertebral column with changes in depth and weight load.** *Journal of Sports Medicine*. 43; Pp 993-1008. 2013.

17. Hoffman et al. **Comparison of Olympic vs traditional power lifting training programs in football players.** *Journal of Strength and Conditioning Research*. 18(1); Pp 129-135. 2004.

18. Hori et al. **Does performance of hang power clean differentiate performance of jumping, sprinting, and changing direction?** *Journal of Strength and Conditioning Research*. 22(2); Pp 412-418. 2008.

19. Linder et al. **Effects of preload 4 repetition maximum on 100-m sprint times in collegiate women.** *Journal of Strength and Conditioning Research*. 24(5); Pp 1184-1190. 2010.

20. Marques and Izquierdo. **Kinetic and kinematic associations between vertical jump performance and 10-m sprint time.** *Journal of Strength and Conditioning Research*. 28(8); Pp 2366-2371. 2014.

21. Osbeck et al. **Validity of Field Testing to Bobsled Start Performance.** *The Journal of Strength & Conditioning Research*. 10(4); Pp 239-245. 1996.

22. Pareja-Blanco et al. **Combined Squat and Light-Load Resisted Sprint Training for Improving Athletic Performance.** *Journal of Strength and Conditioning Research*. 2019.

23. Petrakos et al. **Resisted Sled Sprint Training to Improve Sprint Performance: A Systematic Review.** *Sports Medicine*. 46(3); Pp 381-400. 2016.

24. Robbins DW. **Postactivation potentiation and its practical applicability: a brief review.** *Journal of Strength and Conditioning Research*. 19: Pp 453–45. 2005.

25. Robertson and Fleming. **Kinetics of Broad and Vertical Jumping.** *Canadian Journal of Sport Sciences.* 12(1): Pp 19-23. 1987.
26. Rumpf et al. **Effect of Different Sprint Training Methods on Sprint Performance Over Various Distances: A Brief Review.** *Journal of Strength and Conditioning Research.* 30(6); Pp 1767-1785. 2016.
27. Shea J. *Make a Muscle: Sand as an effective training tool.* *Gatehouse Media.* 2014.
28. Sleivert et al. **The Relationship Between Maximal Jump-Squat Power and Sprint Acceleration in Athletics.** *European Journal of Applied Physiology.* 91(1); Pp 46-52. 2004.
29. Welch et al. **EFFECTS OF THE FRENCH CONTRAST METHOD ON MAXIMUM STRENGTH AND VERTICAL JUMPING PERFORMANCE.** *14th Annual Coaching and Sport Sciences College.* 2019.
30. Yavuz et al. **Kinematic and EMG activities during front and back squat variations in maximum loads.** Journal of Sports Sciences. 33(10); Pp 1058-1066. 2015.
31. Voloshina, A. S., Kuo, A. D., Daley, M. A., & Ferris, D. P. (2013). **Biomechanics and energetics of walking on uneven terrain.** The Journal of experimental biology, 216(Pt 21), 3963–3970.
32. Chien, J. E., & Hsu, W. L. (2018). Effects of Dynamic **Perturbation-Based Training on Balance Control of Community-Dwelling Older Adults.** Scientific reports, 8(1), 17231.
33.

## Chapter 3

1. Alves et al. **Short-term effects of complex and contrast training in soccer players' vertical jump, sprint, and agility abilities.** *Journal of Strength and Conditioning Research.* 24(4); Pp 936-941. 2010.
2. Alves et al. **Postactivation Potentiation Improves Performance in a Resistance Training Session in Trained Men.** *Journal of Strength and Conditioning Research.* 2019.
3. Argus et al. **Kinetic and training comparisons between assisted, resisted, and free countermovement jumps.** *Journal of Strength and Conditioning Research.* 25(8); Pp 2219-2227. 2011.
4. Bauer et al. **Combining higher-load and lower-load resistance training exercises: A systematic review and meta-analysis of findings from complex training studies.** *J Sci Med Sports.* 22(7); Pp 838-851. 2019.

5. Bevan et al. **Influence of postactivation potentiation on sprinting performance in professional rugby players.** *Journal of Strength and Conditioning Research.* 24(3); Pp 701-705. 2010.
6. Bogdanis et al. **Improvement of Long-Jump Performance During Competition Using a Plyometric Exercise.** *International Journal of Sport Physiology and Performance.* 12(2); Pp 235-240. 2017.
7. Bradley-Dade T. **The Effects of Hip-Dominant Post-Activation Potentiation on Broad Jump Performance in Varsity Collegiate Football Players.** *Health Sciences Student Work.* 17. 2019.
8. Bridgeman L. **The Effects of Accentuated Eccentric Loading During Drop Jumps on Strength, Power, Speed and Exercise-Induced Muscle Damage.** *Auckland University of Technology.* 2016.
9. Chatzopoulos et al. **Postactivation potentiation effects after heavy exercise on running speed.** *Journal of Strength and Conditioning Research.* 21(4); Pp 1278-1281. 2007.
10. Chen et al. **Parasympathetic nervous activity mirrors recovery status in weightlifting performance after training.** *Journal of Strength and Conditioning Research.* 25(6); Pp 1546-1552. 2011.
11. Chiu et al. **Postactivation potentiation response in athletic and recreationally trained individuals.** *Journal of Strength and Conditioning Research.* 17(4); Pp 671-677. 2003.
12. Cormier et al. **Complex and Contrast Training: Does Strength and Power Training Sequence Affect Performance-Based Adaptations in Team Sports? A Systematic Review and Meta-analysis.** *Journal of Strength and Conditioning Research.* 2020.
13. Cook et al. **Morning based strength training improves afternoon physical performance in rugby union players.** *Journal of Sci Med Sport.* 17(3); Pp 317-321. 2014.
14. Crow et al. **Low load exercises targeting the gluteal muscle group acutely enhance explosive power output in elite athletes.** *Journal of Strength and Conditioning Research.* 26(2); Pp 438-442. 2012.
15. Cunningham et al. **Postactivation potentiation in professional rugby players: optimal recovery.** *Journal of Strength and Conditioning Research.* 21(4); Pp 1134-1138. 2007.
16. de Freitas et al. **Postactivation potentiation improves acute resistance exercise performance and muscular force in trained men.** *Journal of Strength and Conditioning Research.* doi: 10.1519. Nov 2018.
17. Dinsdale et al. **Eliciting Postactivation Potentiation With Hang Cleans depends on the recovery duration and the individual's 1 repetition maximum strength.** *Journal of Strength and Conditioning Research.* doi: 10.1519. March 2019.
18. Ekstrand et al. **Assessing explosive power production using the backward overhead shot throw and the effects of morning**

resistance exercise on afternoon performance. *Journal of Strength and Conditioning Research.* 27(1); Pp 101-106. 2013.

19. Elbadry et al. **Effect of the French Contrast Method on Explosive Strength and Kinematic Parameters of the Triple Jump Among Female College Athletes**. *Journal of Human Kinetics.* 69; Pp 225-230. 2019.

20. Esformes and Bampouras. **Effect of back squat depth on lower body postactivation potentiation.** *Journal of Strength and Conditioning Research.* 27(11); Pp 2997-3000. 2013.

21. Ford et al. **Use of an overhead goal alters vertical jump performance and biomechanics.** *Journal of Strength and Conditioning Research.* 19(2); Pp 394-399. 2005

22. Ford et al. **Vertical Jump Biomechanics Altered with Virtual Overhead Goal.** *Journal of Applied Biomechanics.* 33(2); Pp 153-159. 2017.

23. Gullich and schmidtbleicher. **Mvc-induced short-term potentiation of explosive force.** *New Sud Athl.* 11; Pp 67-84. 1996.

24. Haff et al. **The temporal profile of postactivation potentiation is related to strength level.** *Journal of Strength and Conditioning Research.* 28(3); Pp 706-715. 2014

25. Hammami et al. **Effects of leg contrast strength training on sprint, agility and repeated change of direction performance in male soccer players.** *Journal of Sports Medicine and Physical Fitness.* 57(11); Pp 1424-1431. 2017.

26. Hancock et al. **Postactivation potentiation enhances swim performance in collegiate swimmers.** *Journal of Strength and Conditioning Research.* 29(4); Pp 912-917. 2015.

27. Hernández-Preciado et al. **Potentiation Effects of the French Contrast Method on Vertical Jumping Ability.** *Journal of Strength and Conditioning Research.* 32(7); Pp 1909-1914. 2018.

28. Iacono et al. **The Effects of Cluster-Set and Traditional-Set Postactivation Potentiation Protocols on Vertical Jump Performance.** *International Journal of Sports Physiology and Performance.* Pp 1-6. October 2019.

29. Jo et al. **Influence of recovery duration after a potentiating stimulus on muscular power in recreationally trained individuals.** *Journal of Strength and Conditioning Research.* 24(2); Pp 343-347. 2010.

30. Kamran et al. **Comparison of Complex Versus Contrast Training on Steroid Hormones and Sports Performance in Male Soccer Players.** *Journal of Chiropractic Medicine.* 18(2); Pp 131-138. 2019.

31. Legrange et al. **Contrast Training Generates Post-Activation Potentiation and Improves Repeated Sprint Ability in Elite Ice Hockey Players.** *International Journal of Exercise Science.* 13(6); Pp 183-196. 2020.

32. Lesinski et al. **Acute effects of postactivation potentiation on strength and speed performance in athletes.** *Sportverletz Sportschaden.* 27(3); Pp 147-155. 2013.
33. Linder et al. **Effects of preload 4 repetition maximum on 100-m sprint times in collegiate women.** *Journal of Strength and Conditioning Research.* 24(5); Pp 1184-1190. 2010.
34. Lum et al. **Effects of various warm-up protocol on special judo fitness test performance.** *Journal of Strength and Conditioning Research.* 33(2); Pp 459-465. 2019.
35. Marshall et al. **Postactivation potentiation and change of direction speed in elite academy rugby players.** *Journal of Strength and Conditioning Research.* 33(6); Pp 1551-1556. 2019.
36. McCann and Flanagan. **The effects of exercise selection and rest interval on postactivation potentiation of vertical jump performance.** *Journal of Strength and Conditioning Research.* 24(5); Pp 1285-1291. 2010.
37. Miarka et al. **Acute effects and postactivation potentiation in the Special Judo Fitness Test.** *Journal of Strength and Conditioning Research.* 25(2); Pp 427-431. 2011.
38. Nickerson et al. **Effect of cluster set warm-up configurations on sprint performance in collegiate male soccer players.** *Applied Physiology, Nutrition, and Metabolism.* 43(6); Pp 625-630. 2018.
39. Rassier et al. **Coexistence of potentiation and fatigue in skeletal muscle.** *Brazilian Journal of Medicine and Biology Research.* 33(5); Pp 499-508. 2000.
40. Read et al. **The effects of postactivation potentiation on golf club head speed.** *Journal of Strength and Conditioning Research.* 27(6); Pp 1579-1582. 2013.
41. Rhea et al. **An examination of training on the VertiMax resisted jumping device for improvements in lower body power in highly trained college athletes.** *Journal of Strength and Conditioning Research.* 22(3); Pp 735-740. 2008.
42. Rhea et al. **The effectiveness of resisted jump training on the VertiMax in high school athletes.** *Journal of Strength and Conditioning Research.* 22(3); Pp 731-734. 2008.
43. Robbins DW. **Postactivation potentiation and its practical applicability: a brief review.** *Journal of Strength and Conditioning Research.* 19: Pp 453–45. 2005.
44. Scott et al. **Complex Training: The Effect of Exercise Selection and Training Status on Postactivation Potentiation in Rugby League Players.** *Journal of Strength and Conditioning Research.* 31(10); Pp 2694-2703. 2017.
45. Seitz et al. **Postactivation Potentiation of Horizontal Jump Performance Across Multiple Sets of a Contrast Protocol.** *Journal of Strength and Conditioning Research.* 30(10); Pp 2733-2740. 2016.

46. Sheppard et al. **The effect of assisted jumping on vertical jump height in high-performance volleyball players.** *Journal of science and medicine in sport* 14; Pp 85-9. 2011.

47. Stockbrugger and Haennel. **Validity and reliability of a medicine ball explosive power test.** *Journal of Strength and Conditioning Research.* 15(4); Pp 431-438. 2001.

48. Strokosch et al. **Impact of Accommodating Resistance in Potentiating Horizontal Jump Performance in Professional Rugby League Players.** *International journal of sports physiology and performance.* 13(9); Pp 1-22. 2018.

49. Swinton et al. **Effect of load positioning on the kinematics and kinetics of weighted vertical jumps.** *Journal of Strength and Conditioning Research.* 26; Pp 906-13. 2012.

50. Tsoukos et al. **Delayed effects of a low-volume, power-type resistance exercise session on explosive performance.** *Journal of Strength and Conditioning Research.* 32(3); Pp 643-650. 2018.

51. Turner et al. **Postactivation potentiation of sprint acceleration performance using plyometric exercise.** *Journal of Strength and Conditioning Research.* 29(2); Pp 343-350. 2015.

52. Wang et al. **Isometric mid-thigh pull correlates with strength, sprint, and agility performance in collegiate rugby union players.** *Journal of Strength and Conditioning Research.* 30(11); Pp 3051-3056. 2016.

53. Weber et al. **Acute effects of heavy-load squats on consecutive squat jump performance.** *Journal of Strength and Conditioning Research.* 22(3); Pp 726-730. 2008.

54. Welch et al. **EFFECTS OF THE FRENCH CONTRAST METHOD ON MAXIMUM STRENGTH AND VERTICAL JUMPING PERFORMANCE.** *14th Annual Coaching and Sport Sciences College.* 2019.

55. Wilson et al. **Meta-analysis of postactivation potentiation and power: effects of conditioning activity, volume, gender, rest periods, and training status.** *Journal of Strength and Conditioning Research.* 27(30); Pp 854-859. 2013.

56. Wong et al. **Sled towing acutely decreases acceleration sprint time.** *Journal of Strength and Conditioning Research.* 31(11); Pp 3046-3051. 2017.

57. Wyland et al. **Postactivation Potentation Effects From Accommodating Resistance Combined With Heavy Back Squats on Short Sprint Performance.** *Journal of Strength and Conditioning Research.* 29(11); Pp 3115-3123. 2015.

58. Yetter, M and Moir, GL. **The acute effects of heavy back and front squats on speed during forty-meter sprint trials.** *Journal of Strength and Conditioning Research.* 22; Pp 159–165. 2008.

# Chapter 4

1. Amalrai A et al. **The Effects of Bioavailable Curcumin (Cureit) on Delayed Onset Muscle Soreness Induced By Eccentric Continuous Exercise: A Randomized, Placebo-Controlled, Double-Blind Clinical Study.** *Journal of Medicine and Food.* 23(5); Pp 545-553. 2020.

2. Ammar A et al. **Pomegranate supplementation accelerates recovery of muscle damage and soreness and inflammatory markers after a weightlifting training session.** *PLoS One.* 11(10):e0160305. 2016.

3. Arent S et al. **The effects of theaflavin-enriched black tea extract on muscle soreness, oxidative stress, inflammation, and endocrine responses to acute anaerobic interval training: a randomized, double-blind, crossover study.** *Journal of International Society of Sports Nutrition.* 7: Pp 11. 2010.

4. Bongers CC et al. **Precooling and percooling (cooling during exercise) both improve performance in the heat: a meta-analytical review.** *British Journal of Sports Medicine.* 49; Pp 377-384. 2015.

5. Bongers C et al. **Cooling interventions for athletes: An overview of effectiveness, physiological mechanisms, and practical considerations.** *Temperature (Austin).* 4(1); Pp 60-78. 2017.

6. Branco BH. **The Effects of Hyperbaric Oxygen Therapy on Post-Training Recovery in Jiu-Jitsu Athletes.** *PLos One.* 11(3); e0150517. 2016.

7. Campbell M et al. **Influence of curcumin on performance and post-exercise recovery.** *Critical Review in Food Science and Nutrition.* doi: 10.1080/10408398.2020.1754754. Pp 1-11. 2020.

8. Chen HY et al. **Effects of caffeine and sex on muscle performance and delayed-onset muscle soreness after exercise-induced muscle damage: a double-blind randomized trial.** *Journal of Applied Physiology (1985).* 127(3); Pp 798-805. 2019.

9. Christina-Souza G et al. **Panax ginseng Supplementation Increases Muscle Recruitment, Attenuates Perceived Effort, and Accelerates Muscle Force Recovery After an Eccentric-Based Exercise in Athletes.** *Journal of Strength and Conditioning Research.* doi: 10.1519/JSC.0000000000003555. 2020.

10. Clarkson P et al. **Muscle soreness and serum creatine kinase activity following isometric, eccentric, and concentric exercise.** *International Journal of Sports Medicine.* 7(3): Pp 152-155. 1986.

11. Corder K et al. **Effects of Short-Term Docosahexaenoic Acid Supplementation on Markers of Inflammation after Eccentric Strength Exercise in Women.** *Journal of Sports Science and Medicine.* 15(1); Pp 176-183. 2016.

12. Cuomo J et al. **Comparative absorption of a standardized curcuminoid mixture and its lecithin formulation.** *Journal of Natural Products.* 74(4);Pp 664-9. 2011

13. Dupuy O, et al. **An Evidence-Based Approach for Choosing Post-exercise Recovery Techniques to Reduce Markers of Muscle Damage, Soreness, Fatigue, and Inflammation: A Systematic Review with Meta-Analysis.** *Frontiers in Physiology.* 9; Pp 403. 2018.

14. Fagiolini A et al. **Lack of interest in sex successfully treated by exposure to bright light.** *European College of Neuropsychopharmacology.* Sept 2016.

15. Fedewa M et al. **Effect of branched-Chain Amino Acid Supplementation on Muscle Soreness following Exercise: A Meta-Analysis.** *International Journal of Vitamin and Nutrition Research.* 89(5-6); Pp 348-356. 2019.

16. Ferraresi C. **Photobiomodulation in human muscle tissue: an advantage in sports performance?** *Journal of Biophotonics.* 9(11-12); Pp 1273-1299. 2016.

17. Georges J et al. **Effects of probiotic supplementation on lean body mass, strength, and power, and health indicators in resistance trained males: a pilot study.** *Journal of the International Society of Sports Nutrition.* 11: Pp 38. 2014.

18. Gleeson M et al. **Daily probiotic's (Lactobacillus casei Shirota) reduction of infection incidence in athletes.** *International Journal of Sport Nutrition and Exercise Metabolism.* 21(1):Pp 55–64. 2011.

19. Goldberg R, Katz J. **A meta-analysis of the analgesic effects of omega-3 polyunsaturated fatty acid supplementation for inflammatory joint pain.** *Pain.* 129(1-2); Pp 210-223. 2007.

20. Gray P et al. **Fish oil supplementation augments post-exercise immune function in young males.** *Brain Behavior and Immunity.* 26(8); Pp 1265-1272. 2012.

21. Hadanny A et al. **Nonhealing Wounds Caused by Brown Spider Bites: Application of Hyperbaric Oxygen Therapy.** *Advanced Skin and Wound Care.* 29(12); Pp 560-566. 2016.

22. Harty P et al. **Nutritional and Supplementation Strategies to Prevent and Attenuate Exercise-Induced Muscle Damage: a Brief Review.** *Sports Medicine Open.* 5(1); 2019.

23. Haywood B et al. **Probiotic supplementation reduces the duration and incidence of infections but not severity in elite rugby union players.** *Journal of Science and Medicine in Sport.* 17(4):Pp 356–360. 2014.

24. Hoffman M et al. **A Placebo-Controlled Trial of Riboflavin for Enhancement of Ultramarathon Recovery**. *Sports Medicine Open*. 3; Pp 14. 2017

25. Ivanov D. *The Science of Winning According to Vasili Alexeyev*. *EliteFTS.com*. 2017.

26. Jager R et al. **Probiotic Bacillus coagulans GBI-30, 6086 reduces exercise-induced muscle damage and increases recovery**. *Peer Reviewed Open Access Journal*. 4: e2276. 2016.

27. Kjellgren A et al. **Effects of flotation-REST on Muscle Tension Pain.** *Pain Research Management*. 6(4); Pp 181-189. 2001.

28. Kjellgren A. **Beneficial effects of treatment with sensory isolation in flotation-tank as a preventive health-care intervention – a randomized controlled pilot trial.** *BMC Complementary and Alternative Medicine*. 14; Pp 417. 2014.

29. Kurz T. *Science of Sports Training*. Stadion Publishing Company. Island Pond, VT. 1991.

30. Lateef F. **Post exercise ice water immersion: Is it a form of active recovery?** *Journal of Emergency Trauma and Shock*. 3(3); Pp 302. 2010.

31. Kuehl, K.S., Perrier, E.T., Elliot, D.L. et al. **Efficacy of tart cherry juice in reducing muscle pain during running: a randomized controlled trial.** J Int Soc Sports Nutr 7, 17 (2010).

32. Lima LC et al. **Consumption of cherries as a strategy to attenuate exercise induced muscle damage and inflammation in humans.** *Nutrition Hospitalaria*. 32(5); Pp 1885-1893. 2015.

33. Lombardi G. **Whole-Body Cryotherapy in Athletes: From Therapy to Stimulation. An Updated Review of the Literature.** *Frotiers in Physiology*. 8; Pp 258. 2017.

34. Maradakis et al. **Caffeine attenuates delayed onset muscle and force loss following eccentric exercise.** *Journal of Pain*. 8(3); 2007

35. Martin-Rincon M et al. **Supplementation with a Mango Leaf Extract (Zynamite®) in Combination with Quercetin Attenuates Muscle Damage and Pain and Accelerates Recovery after Strenuous Damaging Exercise.** *Nutrients*. 12(3); Pp 614. 2020.

36. McLeay Y et al. **Effect of New Zealand blueberry consumption on recovery from eccentric exercise-induced muscle damage.** *Journal of International Society of Sports and Nutrition*. 9(1); Pp 19. 2012.

37. Miller PC et al. **The effects of protease supplementation on skeletal muscle function and DOMS following downhill running.** *Journal of Sports Sciences*. 22(4); Pp 365–72. 2004.

38. Milewski, M. D., Skaggs, D. L., Bishop, G. A., Pace, J. L., Ibrahim, D. A., Wren, T. A., & Barzdukas, A. (2014). **Chronic lack of sleep is**

associated with increased sports injuries in adolescent athletes. Journal of pediatric orthopedics, 34(2), 129–133.

39. Oschman JL. **Perspective: assume a spherical cow: the role of free or mobile electrons in bodywork, energetic and movement therapies.** Journal of Bodywork and Movement Therapies. 2008;12(1):40–57.

40. Ramos-Campo D et al. **Supplementation of Re-Esterified Docosahexaenoic and Eicosapentaenoic Acids Reduce Inflammatory and Muscle Damage Markers after Exercise in Endurance Athletes: A Randomized, Controlled Crossover Trial.** *Nutrients.* 12(3); Pp 719. 2020.

41. Righi NC et al. **Effects of vitamin C on oxidative stress, inflammation, muscle soreness, and strength following acute exercise: meta-analyses of randomized clinical trials.** *European Journal of Nutrition.* doi: 10.1007/s00394-020-02215-2. 2020.

42. Salarkia N et al. **Effects of probiotic yogurt on performance, respiratory and digestive systems of young adult female endurance swimmers: a randomized controlled trial.** *Medical Journal of The Islamic Republic of Iran.* 27(3): Pp 141–146. 2013.

43. Smith N et al. **Ozone therapy: an overview of pharmacodynamics, current research, and clinical utility.** *Medical Gas Research.* 7(3); Pp 212-219. 2017.

44. Stock M et al. **The Time Course of Short-Term Hypertrophy in the Absence of Eccentric Muscle Damage.** *European Journal of Applied Physiology.* 117(5); Pp 989-1004. 2017.

45. Tinsely G et al. **Effects of Fish Oil Supplementation on Postresistance Exercise Muscle Soreness.** *Journal of Dietary Supplements.* 14(1); 2017.

46. Tsuchiya Y et al. **Low Dose of β-Hydroxy-β-Methylbutyrate (HMB) Alleviates Muscle Strength Loss and Limited Joint Flexibility following Eccentric Contractions.** *Journal of American College of Nutrition.* doi: 10.1080/07315724.2020.1752330. Pp 1-8. 2020.

47. Yarizadh H et al. **The Effect of L-Carnitine Supplementation on Exercise-Induced Muscle Damage: A Systematic Review and Meta-Analysis of Randomized Clinical Trials.** *Journal of the American College of Nutrition.* 39(5); Pp 457-468. 2020.

48. Williams E, Heckman S. **The local diurnal variation of cloud electrification and the global diurnal variation of negative charge on the Earth.** Journal of Geophysical Research. 1993;98(3):5221–5234

49. Watkins C, Archer D, et al. **Determlateefination of ea as a Measure of Neuromuscular Readiness and Fatigue.** *Journal of Strength and Conditioning Research.* 31(12); Pp 3305-3310. 2017.

50. Woodyard C. **Exploring the therapeutic effects of yoga and its ability to increase quality of life.** *International Journal of Yoga.* 4(2); Pp 49-54. 2011.

51. Zainuddin Z et al. **Light Concentric Exercise Has a Temporarily Analgesic Effect on Delayed-Onset Muscle Soreness, but No Effect on Recovery From Eccentric Exercise.** *Applied Physiology in Nutrition and Metabolism.* 31(2); Pp 126-134. 2006.

52. Zheng-Tao L et al. **Omega-3 Polyunsaturated Fatty Acid Supplementation for Reducing Muscle Soreness after Eccentric Exercise: A Systematic Review and Meta-Analysis of Randomized Controlled Trials.** Biomedical Research International. 8062017. 2020.

Printed in Great Britain
by Amazon

16561108R00157